D1302387

COLLEGE SUCCESS:
A CONCISE PRACTICAL GUIDE

Sixth Edition

David L. Strickland, MA

Carol J. Strickland, PhD, RN

BVT Publishing
Better textbooks, better prices
www.BVTPublishing.com

Publisher and Marketing Manager: Richard Schofield

Managing Editor: Joyce Bianchini

Copy Editor: Anne Schofield

Production and Fulfillment Manager: Janai Bryand

Cover and Interior Design: Esther Scannell

Typesetting Manager: Rhonda Minnema

Proofreader: Nancy E. Williams

Pre-Production Manager: Shannon Waters

For information, address BVT Publishing, LLC, P.O. Box 492831, Redding, CA 96049-2831

Some ancillaries, including electronic and printed components, may not be available to customers outside of the United States.

Photo Credits: Cover and feature heading icon images from Shutterstock, iStock, and Getty Images.

eBook ISBN: 978-1-62751-361-6

Loose-leaf ISBN: 978-1-62751-358-6

Soft Cover ISBN: 978-1-62751-359-3

Textbook-Plus Bundle ISBN: 978-1-62751-362-3

CONTENTS

Preface to the Sixth Edition

To the Student

Welcome to College!

College Success: A Concise Practical Guide is especially designed to help you to succeed in college. It contains ten brief—but rich—chapters on topics proven to make a difference for academic success. This book is written by two professors who have over thirty-six years of combined teaching experience. They have taught in small, two-year colleges as well as in large public and private universities. The book can be used alone or in conjunction with a course that focuses on student success in college.

Following are ways in which you will benefit from reading this book and completing all of the assignments:

- You will learn to approach the challenge of college with a **perspective** and **attitude** that will help you be successful—not only in college but in life after graduation.
- You will learn **techniques** that will help you plan, organize, listen, learn, read, and write in college.
- You will learn how to connect with **people** on campus who will support your success.
- You will learn how to connect with **resources** on campus that will support your success.

If this book is used while you are taking a course about being successful in college, read the chapters thoughtfully before your instructor discusses them in class. You will be glad you did.

How This Book Works

College Success includes exercises and assignments that you can complete on your own, or as part of a course. The classroom is a great place to discuss techniques for success, and your new college experiences with your instructor and your peers. A student-success class can be like a support group for new college students.

The Chapter Roadmap

Each chapter begins with the *Chapter Roadmap* page. The chapter roadmap includes a brief abstract or summary of the chapter, a list of the learning goals for that chapter, and a checklist to help you work through the chapter.

The Learning Goals

One of the most important features of this textbook, and possibly any textbook, is the list of learning goals. The learning goals are a series of statements that describe what you should be able to do after you have read and studied the chapter. These goals help you to identify what aspects of the chapter are most important; therefore, if used properly, they can help you sharpen the focus of your study. In a well-designed course, the learning goals and the questions you see on exams will be linked. That is, the exam questions will be specifically designed to measure whether you have successfully achieved the learning goals. Thus, you could use the learning goals to develop a study guide that would enable you to efficiently prepare for exams. We will describe how to do this in more detail under the section titled "How to Use the Study Guide." The checklist will help you connect the learning goals to the study guide pages found at the end of each chapter. The study guide pages, if used properly, will help you identify and learn the important concepts of the chapter. Those concepts are the same ones that you can expect to see represented on exams.

The Checklist

The checklist presents a series of activities to complete as you study the chapter. You will benefit most if you *complete the activities in the order in which they appear* since they are deliberately ordered to give you the best learning experience. For example, the first item on the list is the "Critical Thinking Activity." This should be done before you read the chapter because it will be referenced later; if you have completed it prior to reading, you will better understand the chapter. The same principle applies to the second item on the checklist: compiling a series of questions about the learning goals that you can reference as you read.

Critical Thinking Activity

As mentioned earlier, immediately following the Chapter Roadmap page is a Critical Thinking Activity. Remember that college-level study is more about thinking and understanding than about memorization. Some memorization may still be necessary—especially when you encounter concepts that are completely new to you; however, thinking critically about and analyzing those concepts are central to a college education.

Please note that the Critical Thinking Activity is the first item on the checklist, and is designed to be completed before you read the chapter. You will find that these activities are referred to later in the chapter; in order to understand the reference, you will need to have completed the activity.

Reading Comprehension Questions

As you read, you will periodically come across *Reading Comprehension Questions.* There are four types of these questions in each chapter. When you encounter one of these questions, pause from your reading and try to answer it. When you finish the chapter, check your answers for all four questions against the answer key located in the Appendix. If you missed any of the questions, go back and review that section of the chapter and try to figure out why.

This activity is designed to help you improve your reading comprehension in four areas: 1) vocabulary, 2) literal comprehension, 3) inferential comprehension, and 4) analysis. You can use the table in the Appendix to check your answers and assess your strengths and weakness. Simply record your answers and check them using the table. Then use the table to count the number of questions you got correct in each of the four categories. This will give you a general idea of which types of reading comprehension you do best and which types you may need to work on.

Chapter Summary

The brief chapter summary can be used to quickly grasp the topics that will be covered. Reading it, and the learning goals, before you begin the chapter will create a framework for all of the information to follow, so that you will learn and remember more.

Review Questions

Near the end of each chapter you will find a page of *review questions.* There will be five true/false questions. You should mark your answer and then, in the space provided, write your rationale, (reason) for selecting true or false. If you are using this book for a student-success course, then your instructor will have the answer key for the chapter review questions.

Assignments

One or more practical assignments can be found at the end of each chapter (with directions provided). If you are taking a student-success class, your professor may assign some of these for you to do as part of your grade.

How to Use the Study Guide

Each chapter has a *study guide,* designed to help you understand and discuss material from the chapter. As already mentioned, the learning goals for each chapter are listed at the beginning (on the Chapter Roadmap page). These goals are then repeated on the top of each study guide page. The learning goals tell you what is important in the chapter. If you want to seriously study the chapter and accomplish the learning goals, you will need to do more than simply read the learning goals. You will need to break them down into one or more questions.

Step 1: Convert the Learning Goals into Questions Before You Read the Chapter.

The learning goals are expressed as statements. Therefore, if you want to make sure that you thoroughly understand each goal, you will have to first convert them into questions. Do this *before* you read the chapter in the space provided for you on the study guide pages. Simply *write the questions in the left-hand column* of the study guide page. Look at Figure 1 as an example. The fictional student, Sharon Cooper, has converted Learning Goal #1 for Chapter 5 into five different questions. Each of these questions will help Sharon with a different aspect of the goal. Notice how the questions are broken down into the *smallest parts* possible. Thus, there are many questions covering just one goal. You should try to break down the goal into *as many questions* as you can. This will allow you to focus on the details of the goal, rather than just skimming the chapter's contents.

Figure 1 Example of Study Guide Page Based on a Lesson Objective

Name: *Sharon Cooper*

Chapter Five

Study Guide

Chapter 5, Goal 1: The student will be able to compare and contrast the focus-on-grades approach with the focus-on-learning approach.

Questions	Answers & Notes
1. What is the focus-on-grades approach?	*It is an approach to learning in which the student thinks of the grade as something separate from learning. Given this focus, he or she attempts to achieve the desired grade with the least investment possible.*
2. What is the focus-on-learning approach?	*It is an approach to learning in which the student seeks to learn as much as he or she can in the course.*
3. How are the focus-on-grades and the focus-on-learning approaches similar? (compare)	*These approaches are similar in that they are both ways in which students approach the way they learn in college. They both result in grades that are reflective of the approach taken.*
4. How are the focus-on-grades and the focus on learning approaches different? (contrast)	*These approaches are different in that the student is trying to learn at a different level, resulting in good grades if the student has learned but not necessarily a good grade if the student has not learned at a deeper level. The focus-on-grades approach involves focusing on what is on a test and on shortcuts that the student can use to learn quickly. The focus-on-learning approach involves focusing on learning the most a student can learn in the course and on what the most important material to learn is.*
5. What are at least two ways in which the focus-on-learning approach is more effective than the focus-on-grades approach?	*The focus-on-learning approach is more effective because it results in deeper learning than the focus-on-grades approach. Deeper learning means that the student will retain the information for the long-term, and not just for a short-term test. In addition, the focus-on-learning approach automatically results in higher exam scores because the student has learned the material he or she needs to know.*

Step 2: Read the Chapter.

Once you have clarified exactly what it is that you need to learn from the chapter, you are ready to *start reading*. As you read, *keep the learning goal questions in mind*. When you encounter information pertaining to one of your questions, you should make a note of it. Some students like to highlight the information and then write a note for themselves in the margin reminding them why it is highlighted.

Step 3: Answer Your Study Guide Questions.

Once you understand the answers to your study guide questions, you should record the answers in the right-hand column of the study guide (see Figure 1). Why? This will allow you to create a series of questions and answers that you can use as a study and regulation tool (see Step 5 below).

Step 4: Read Your Study Guide Pages.

With your study guide completed, you can now study simply by reading through it. It is often helpful to read the pages aloud as a study activity. Read and repeat. You should read your study guide on a regular basis throughout the semester, and if you are preparing for an exam based on the learning goals.

Step 5: Use the Study Guide to Test Yourself.

Testing yourself as a part of your regular study routine is called **regulation**. This is a key to success, especially if you are going to have an exam based on the learning goals. Hold a blank piece of paper in your hand and use it to cover the right column (the answers). Then read the first question to yourself. Try to answer it. After you state your answer, slide the blank page down to reveal the answer and check your progress. Repeat this with the next questions, and so on, until you finish all of the questions. Note any questions that you miss and spend additional time studying those before your next regulation session. Use this regulation strategy on a regular basis throughout the semester. Then, on the night before an exam, you will not need to stay up long hours cramming. By then, all you will probably need to do is read your study guide and regulate one last time. After a good night's sleep, you can wake up refreshed and go tackle the exam with confidence. If you regulate on a very regular basis, as we have described here, you will be so familiar with the most important questions of the course that by the time you take the exam, you are sure to score very high. What's more, the knowledge you have gained will be imprinted in your long-term memory, where it will serve you for years to come.

BVT Lab

Student study resources for this book are also available at www.BVTLab.com. These resources are included with certain printed formats of the book. Where applicable, a single-use access code is included inside the back cover. These online resources may also be purchased directly from the website.

The online resources include:

- An eBook (both downloadable and web-view versions)
- Practice quizzes
- Flashcards
- PowerPoint slides.

We hope this book will help you to navigate through your first year of college as successfully as possible! Feel free to contact either one of us with questions or suggestions for improving this book.

David L. Strickland (dstrick@ega.edu) & Carol J. Strickland (ccornwel@gmail.com)

To the Instructor

This book was written with the student in mind and has been developed as a comprehensive reading and study guide, that both student and instructor can use in a course focusing on college success. The book is also written so that students can use it independently, in case they are not enrolled in a college-success course. The book is learner-centered, and will hopefully capture the interest of students and keep them engaged throughout the semester.

This text has several features that we hope will provide additional resources and enrichment—to assist the student in becoming a successful college scholar. Many of the features and resources can also be useful in the classroom as activities that will provide valuable experiences for your students. These include a) Chapter Roadmaps (which comprise a brief chapter summary, chapter learning goals, and a study checklist), b) Critical Thinking Activities; c) a comprehensive test bank, d) reading comprehension questions, e) links to websites that complement the chapter, f) study guide pages for each chapter, and g) learning activities and assignments designed specifically for each chapter—all in a student-friendly format.

Student-Friendly Format

This text is written in plain, everyday language that is designed to be student-friendly and easily understood. Multiple features were designed to be helpful to the student as he or she progresses through the text.

Chapter Roadmaps

Chapter Roadmaps are located at the beginning of each chapter; they include an overview of the entire chapter along with learning goals and a checklist designed to help the student focus on the most important aspects as they work through each chapter. The learning goals presented in the Chapter Roadmap are linked to the study guide (where they are repeated).

Critical Thinking Activities

Immediately following the roadmap page is a Critical Thinking Activity. These are intended to be completed by the student *prior* to reading the chapter. Note that this order is reinforced in the checklist. Each activity poses a problem or issue that will stimulate further critical thinking by students, and help mentally prepare them to get the most from the chapter. This feature was developed in order to engage the student in deeper thought about a topic and may, in some cases, be used by the instructor in the classroom as a discussion starter.

Test Questions

Test questions were developed to reinforce chapter concepts and measure progress toward the learning goals, as well as to verify that the students have read the chapter. This test bank is available to the instructor for use in quizzes and/or exams, and can be found at the faculty ancillary website for this text. The test bank includes questions in multiple formats (including multiple choice, true/false, short answer, and essay) for each chapter.

Reading Comprehension Questions

Four questions have been included throughout each chapter so that students can self-regulate their reading comprehension. The questions have been designed to assess the following four major aspects of reading: 1) vocabulary, 2) literal comprehension, 3) inferential comprehension, and 4) analysis. In the Appendix, there is a table that can be used by the student to record his or her answers and to check them against an answer sheet. The table then allows students to tally the number of questions they got correct in each of the four categories, giving them a general idea of their reading strengths and weaknesses.

Links to Websites

Links to relevant websites are included in each chapter. They are designed to provide additional information, and to pique students' interest about the topic.

Study Guide Pages

At the end of each chapter, there are study guide pages based on the learning goals. Space is provided for student-generated questions and answers. Please refer to *How to Use the Study Guide* (in the section titled To the Student) for more detailed information.

Learning Activities and Assignments

The learning activities and assignments include specific interactive exercises that encourage the student to apply concepts covered in each chapter.

Ancillaries

We have created the following ancillary package for instructors:

Instructor's Manual

The instructor's manual provides many resources for the instructor—including teaching suggestions and strategies for each chapter, example syllabi, model course design suggestion, instructor checklists, student handouts, and instructor links to online resources.

PowerPoint Slides

PowerPoint slides are provided for each chapter.

Test Bank Files

The test bank includes questions for each chapter and is available in three database formats: Respondus, Excel, and as a comma separated text file. The questions from the test bank are also available as an MS Word or text document.

We hope this textbook will be valuable to you as you teach students the tools and strategies necessary to succeed in college and beyond. Please let us know if you have suggestions for improvement or other comments. We encourage you to contact BVT if you wish to adapt this book specifically to your own institution's needs, perhaps by adding or modifying portions.

David L. Strickland (dstrick@ega.edu)
Carol J. Strickland (ccornwel@ega.edu)

To the Administrator

Some background information about how this textbook was developed may be of interest to administrators. The personalized, versatile, and cost-effective features of the book are of particular interest.

Our Experience

The institution where David taught had a one-credit-hour orientation course that was required for students who had tested into learning support classes (such as learning support math or learning support English). Typically, only underprepared students enrolled in the course (as the orientation course was not otherwise required). However, administrators and faculty were seeking practical, effective and cost-efficient ways to improve learning and to increase retention, completion, and graduation rates. It was clear that a majority of the new students entering college had weak or non-existent organizational skills and poor study strategies. The approach and strategies most commonly employed by students (such as cramming for exams as the primary or sole method of study) appeared to be ineffective and sometimes counterproductive. This was true for students in general—not just for those who had lower entrance exam scores.

We decided to create an orientation course similar to a first-year experience course that would be required for all new students. The instructor would serve as a mentor, and the students in the class would serve as a support group for one another during their first semester. Topics addressed by the course would include basic study skills as well as an orientation to campus policies and procedures. Initially, the course was taught by volunteer faculty as a part of their service to the college. For the first year, we adopted a textbook that was similar in design to the textbooks used in other courses and typical of those used for student success at that time.

Evaluation of the program after the first year revealed a few problems with the textbook. The cost of the book to students was prohibitively high (over $100), and we found that instructors used very little of the book in their classes (usually only about one chapter). So we began looking for a solution. The second year we tried to run the program without a book, but we found it ineffective and difficult to standardize around central objectives. Finally, I suggested that we produce our own textbook that would address a simple list of core competencies and that would be personalized to our institution and the specific needs of our students. I volunteered to write most of it, and we discovered that BVT could help us publish it for less cost than it would be for us to produce it in-house. We personalized the text to our institution, and we decided that it could serve as an orientation manual, a textbook for study skills, and a day planner that the student could use to organize his or her studies—not only the first year of college but also every year until graduation. Important college events and deadlines were already printed on the calendar within the book.

One of the ways in which we made the first edition of the college success book very cost-effective was to include, within the book, approximately forty pages of handouts that were formerly distributed during new-student orientation. In this way we were able to capture the cost of paper, printing, copying, collating, and so on since those orientation handouts were included in our new textbook at no additional cost. The textbooks were distributed to students during orientation, and the portion of the text containing the information from the previous handouts was used for instruction during orientation. The students were told that the remaining pages of the same book would serve as the textbook for the required student-success course during their first semester.

Customization for Your Campus

College Success: A Concise Practical Guide can be easily customized for your campus, and even for different courses and disciplines on your campus. You can include an appendix with all of your printed orientation materials. These can be perforated pages in the bound book, or color-coded pages in the loose-leaf format.

Other customizations that you might consider are:

- Rearranging the chapter order
- Deleting unwanted chapters
- Adding chapters with your own content
- Modifying any of the text or illustrations throughout the text
- Creating additional assignments or in-class exercises
- Creating additional lab content or student resources

Please contact BVT Publishing for further information on customization.

Acknowledgments

We wish to acknowledge the input and contributions of many people who had a role or made a contribution to the preparation of this book. We extend our thanks to our colleagues at East Georgia State College, who have offered encouragement, inspiration, and many great ideas that we have attempted to include in the book. Special thanks to those instructors who have taught Student Success and have provided us with valuable feedback. Certain colleagues have been especially influential: David Altamirano, Ed Bayens, Larry Braddy, Alan Brasher, Carol Bray, John Bressler, Angie Brown, Randy Carter, Sally Cook, Ron Conner, Val Czerny, Mark Dallas, Jeff Edgens, Elizabeth Gilmer, Tim Goodman, Raymond Hayes, Ken Homer, Pat Homer, Jeff Howell, Courtney Joiner, Bob March, Walter Mason, Dee McKinney, Caroline McMillan, John Neighbors, Bob Neil, Anna Marie Reich, Sandra Sharman, Janet Stracher, Tommy Upchurch, Raleigh Way, and Eric Wruck. We would like to give many thanks to the BVT family, without whose help and guidance this book would not have been possible. Thanks to Nate Shankles and Richard Schofield for providing a way for our vision to go forward and to Joyce Bianchini, Janai Bryand, Esther Scannell, Rhonda Minnema, Nancy E. Williams, and Shannon Waters who helped make our vision become a reality! Many thanks and congratulations to all of you!

About the Authors

DAVID L. STRICKLAND, MA, is the director of the Student Success Program and an associate professor of sociology at East Georgia State College. He is co-author of an introductory sociology textbook, *My Sociology,* now in its second edition. He is the author of the freshman orientation course textbook at East Georgia State College, *College Success: A Concise Practical Guide* (formerly *Student Success*), now in its sixth edition. In addition to writing, he has taught college courses full time for more than eighteen years. During that time he also served for three years as the director of institutional research for the college. Prior to teaching sociology, he conducted grant-funded health care research at the Center for Rural Health and Research at Georgia Southern University and published numerous articles and chapters on the sociology of health care. He has been a pioneer in the area of online instruction and served as a co-author for the eCore version of *Introduction to Sociology,* which was used by the thirty-four institutions of the University of Georgia. Strickland credits some of his insights regarding orientation to college to the fact that he, like a large number of the students that he teaches, was a first-generation college graduate.

CAROL J. STRICKLAND, PhD, RN, is retired from teaching but served for seven years as associate professor of nursing and director of nursing research at Georgia Southern University School of Nursing in Statesboro, Georgia, and for fourteen years as assistant professor of nursing at the University of Rochester School of Nursing in Rochester, New York, where she received her PhD in nursing. Her interests and clinical experiences are in the area of psychiatric mental health nursing, combining her knowledge of nursing with that of the neuropsychological and neuroimmunological functioning of the human brain. She has published numerous articles in the area of psychiatric mental health nursing practice, psychoneuroimmunology, and sociology. Strickland states that her knowledge of first year experiences comes both from having served as an instructor/mentor in a first-year experience course at the University of Rochester, and from immersion in the literature. She has gained insights into the value of having a book designed to guide the mentorship process that is so essential to helping students transition from high school to college. "In this way, we pass on core competencies and the knowledge to facilitate educated, visionary, and dedicated scholars who will be the leaders, teachers, and mentors of tomorrow."

What Students Have Said About College Success

" "

To be honest, in the beginning of this course, I deemed it unnecessary for me to take this course. I thought the lessons in this course were things that I would already know, but I have honestly learned so much. My favorite and most informative lesson is Designing Your Long-Term Graduation Plan. I really got to see just how long it will take me to graduate, and it gave me the ability to view what classes I should take together and the ones I shouldn't due to the difficulty of each. I also liked the Focus-on-Learning Assignment because it gave me a sense of the difference between focusing on grades and learning. To be honest, I didn't know there was much of a difference between the two. I discovered that many students simply focus on grades because grades equal diplomas and students rarely become interested in actually learning the material. I also learned that memorizing material doesn't always guarantee actually grasping the material at hand. I have applied many of the online assignments to my daily use.

The Student Success course helped me in many ways. In high school I was the student who skimmed through textbooks for answers, procrastinated down to the last second to complete projects, and did very little outside research once class was over. This semester (Fall 2013) actually is not my first college semester, but it is my first successful college semester. My first attempt at college was pathetic, to say the least. I was constantly behind, confused, and frustrated. I surely could have used a class like this back then, and now that I have taken Student Success, I feel far more confident and prepared to earn my degree.

The Student Success handbook includes many easy-to-use templates and organizers to help students form and follow study plans. I have even mapped out every class I will take up until I earn my degree from East Georgia College. If you had told me I would be this organized and on-beat a year ago, I wouldn't have believed you, but here I am. I now understand that by trying to "just get by," I was being academically dishonest and doing a great disservice to myself.

Now I'm taking my time when I'm reading for class. I look up words I don't know. I plan out my projects the day I get them and stick to my plan. I do extra research on things we discuss in class. I am excited about earning my degree, and I am doing all that I can to utilize my resources and get the highest education I can. I am no longer trying to "make the grade"; I am trying to learn. That is what this class did for me, and I am very thankful for the change.

Student Success has helped me in one HUGE way. Over the last few chapters of the textbook, I have realized how I have cheated myself out of the joy of one of my classes. I owe that professor an apology. I have made B's in his class. I will not fail the course. I have not been bored. The honest truth is that I have been lazy and have procrastinated. I have a busy family life but I KNOW I could have done more! I could have made a very high A and left the course with such a better understanding than what I have.

This book made so many good points that new college students need to recognize immediately if they want to be successful in college, attain a degree, or further their education. The first thing would be to understand that it was a choice to come to college, but no one will hold your hand, as they did in High School, to guide you to a degree. Another big take-away is, once the decision has been made to attend college, you have to make college and your studies a priority—not just try and fit it into or around your already busy schedule.

The chapter that was most helpful for me and I expect to be using was...the information about ... the library ... and writing styles. It's good to always have those websites that I go back and look at when I am writing any kind of paper for class. I really enjoyed this course and think that everyone who attends college can benefit from this course.

When you go to college, you have to plan. I have found that making and following the guidelines in advance (long-term plans) helps in seeing what is coming up and will help you prepare for the week better. This will show you how you need to break down your assignments so that you can work along on them and not cram for them the night before the assignment is due. I think that this is the best tool that I will continue to use in the future and that it is a tool ALL students should use.

College is nothing like high school. Even though I was in the top county when it came to education, I could still get away with turning in a paper late or convincing the teacher to give me a little extra points on an exam. In college it is literally all up to me when it comes to assignment grades and exam scores and it's tough. I definitely have had to give up something I wanted to do to tend to my schoolwork. I know in the end all this schoolwork will reward me.

Things such as how to plan my study calendar, how to write a research paper, how to deal with my college-debt problem, and how to set up appointments with my professors are just a few examples of what I have learned from [this book] ...

This book helped me to see that being organized and keeping up with my class assignments really does pay off. Student Success has helped me become a better student by being prepared and having a study plan so that I can do my best on each test.

It couldn't be explained any easier. ... It taught me a lot about preparing myself and planning to study for different classes. It even showed me how to write the professor. It shows me how much time I have to study for each class and how to plan a schedule that works for my schoolwork and personal life.

I just wanted to thank you for all of the help and knowledge that you gave me in your student-success class! I understand now how important all of your info is to me! Your class was very helpful, so teach it the same every semester for your upcoming students. They will really appreciate it in the end! Thank you again!

Chapter 1 Roadmap

Adjusting to College: We're Not in High School Anymore!

In this chapter you will learn about some of the ways in which college is different from high school, and you will gain a better understanding of what will be expected of you. This chapter also describes how this book is designed to help you do your best in college and ultimately reach your goal of earning a college education and a degree.

This chapter roadmap page presents the formal learning goals for this chapter; in addition, there is a checklist that you should follow as you read and study the chapter. You will benefit most if you complete the activities in the order that they are listed.

Student Learning Goals for This Chapter

After completing this chapter you should be able to do the following:

1. Describe the ways in which high school and college are different.
2. Anticipate many of the challenges associated with attending college.
3. Define success in college in terms of both certification and qualification.

Checklist for This Chapter

Target date/ deadline	Check when completed	Activity
________	❑	1. Complete Critical Thinking Activity 1.1.
________	❑	2. Convert the learning goals (above) to questions that you can answer as you read the chapter. Write your questions on the study guide pages near the end of this chapter.
________	❑	3. Read the chapter.
________	❑	4. Try to answer the reading comprehension questions as you come to them in the chapter. Check each answer by comparing it to the list of correct answers in the back of the book. If any answer was not correct, then review the passages preceding the question to see why you missed the question.
________	❑	5. Answer the questions you created in Step 2 of this list. Once completed, these answered questions will be your study guide.
________	❑	6. Complete Review Questions 1.1.
________	❑	7. Complete Assignment 1.1 (Record of Grades).
________	❑	8. Review what you have learned from this chapter.

CRITICAL THINKING ACTIVITY 1.1

What Is Success in College?

Before you read this chapter—and without looking anything up on the Internet or elsewhere—use the space provided on this page to write your own definition of success in college.

What is success in college?

Adjusting to College:
We're Not in High School Anymore!

Some people dream of success while others wake up and work hard at it.

Winston Churchill [1]

For many first-time college students, college is like a magical land filled with new wonders and experiences. Perhaps you, like most students, are experiencing greater autonomy and independence than you ever have before. Surely some adjustment will be necessary to keep your balance. Most students realize that this is true of their social lives—but they may not immediately realize how much college differs from high school academically.

This book will help you successfully transition from high school to college. It covers principles, attitudes, and behaviors that will help you maximize your college experience, reach learning outcomes, stay in your academic program, and graduate. Chapter 1 begins by describing some of the ways in which college is different from high school academically.

1.1 High School Is Not College

High school and college are different in many ways. This is not to say that high school is inferior but rather to help students identify and address the challenges unique to college. There is a misconception that college is like "Grade 13"; but students who believe that college is like high school do not perform as well as students who have more accurate expectations. High school may have prepared you academically for college, but the norms (the way things are done) in college are often very different from what you have experienced in high school. What, specifically, are the differences? Table 1.1 presents some of the most important ones.

Table 1.1 High School versus College * Information paraphrased from multiple sources

Characteristic	High School Model	College Model
Venue for Learning	Most learning occurs in class. Students may study outside class as little as one to two hours a week, and this may be mostly last-minute test preparation.	Most learning occurs outside of class. On average, Students will need to study about two hours outside of class for each hour spent in class.
Schedule	The student attends classes back-to-back for about six hours each day (thirty to thirty five hours per week).	The student must create his or her own schedule. Most classes do not meet every day. There may be many unscheduled hours between classes. Class times vary throughout the day and evening. The student spends only twelve to seventeen hours each week in class.
Role of the Instructor	Teachers are directive and nurturing.	Professors expect the student to be independent and to take personal responsibility for learning.
Office Hours	Teachers do not keep office hours. Instead, they answer questions and offer help to students in class.	Professors schedule regular office hours in order to meet with students individually. Scheduled office hours are usually posted in the syllabus, on the professor's website, and on the office door. (The syllabus is a document that contains lots of important information about the expectations of the course.) You are not interrupting or bothering professors when you meet with them during their office hours. That time has been set aside especially for you. You could just drop by the office; however, if you have a serious question, you should make an appointment so that the time slot will be reserved for you.
Reading Requirements	The student seldom needs to read anything more than once, and sometimes listening in class is enough.	The amount of reading assigned by professors may be large. The student must review class notes and text material regularly. Preparation for exams typically requires multiple reviews of all course materials.
Presentation of Material	Teachers present the material at a slower pace, and the presentation is designed to support the textbook.	Professors present the material at a more rapid pace, and their presentation is designed to supplement the text. Professors often expect you to study the book on your own—and then they will add to or explain it.
Frequency of Testing	There is frequent testing. Therefore, the student is required to master only a small amount of the total course material for any single exam.	Testing is less frequent (often limited to a midterm and final). Therefore, the student must be prepared to demonstrate mastery of a much larger amount of material for a single exam.
Extra Credit	High school grades may be derived not only from exams but also from other assignments. Consistently good homework grades or extra credit assignments might be used to compensate for poor performance on exams and raise your course grade.	College grades are usually derived from exams and major papers. Typically, there is limited opportunity (or none) to earn additional points toward the semester grade. It is important that you determine how each of your courses will be graded. This information is provided in the syllabus.

Sources: College Board. (2009). *College survival tips: making the transition.* Retrieved May 17, 2009, from http://www.collegeboard.com/student/plan/college-success/963.html; C. Partlow (2009, March 16). *How is college different from high school?* Retrieved May 17, 2009, from Montgomery College, Montgomery County, Maryland, First-Year Experience Program website; http://www.montgomerycollege.edu/fye/highschooldiffcollege.html; N. Rockler-Gladen (2007). *High school versus college life: A freshman year guide to different student academic expectations.* Retrieved May 17, 2009, from http://collegeuniversity.suite101.com/article.cfm/high_school_versus_college; D. Thompson (2011). What's the best investment: Stocks, bonds, homes … or college? *The Atlantic.* Retrieved April 30, 2012, from http://www.theatlantic.com/business/archive/2011/06/whats-the-best-investment-stocks-bonds-homes-or-college/241056/

Montgomery College's *The First-Year Experience Program* website offers the following five guiding principles based on the differences between high school and college:[2]

1. As a high school student, you were probably told what to do and were corrected if you did not do it, but in college "you are expected to take responsibility for what you do and don't do, as well as for the consequences of your decisions."[2]

2. In high school you were probably told what you needed to learn from the reading assignment in class, but in college it is "up to you to read and understand the assigned material [because the] lectures and assignments proceed from the assumption that you've already done so."[2]

3. High school was primarily about learning facts and skills, but "college is a learning environment in which you take responsibility for thinking through and applying what you have learned."[2]
4. High school focused on "the ability to reproduce what you were taught in the form in which it was presented to you, or to solve the kinds of problems you were shown how to solve."[2] In college, however, "mastery is often seen as the ability to apply what you've learned to new situations or to solve new kinds of problems."[2]
5. In high school you may have been rewarded for a "good-faith effort," but in college "results count … good-faith effort will not substitute for results in the grading process."[2]

You have probably begun to formulate a pretty good picture of how the college experience will be different from the high school experience after reading Table 1.1. Consider the practical implications of some of those differences. What are the implications of increased freedom and responsibility? What changes will you have to make to the way you study and prepare for exams or other assessments? How will your reading load be different? What will professors expect of you?

Reading Comprehension Question 1.1 (Knowledge)

Which of the following are ways in which college is different from high school?

a. In high school, teachers are directive and nurturing.
b. In college, the amount of reading assigned by professors can be very large.
c. In college, professors expect you to study the text on your own.
d. All of the above

1.2 College Involves Freedom and Responsibility

It is great to be an adult in college with the independence and freedom to make your own decisions about how you spend your time. The downside is that you are now the only person responsible for those decisions.

When you were younger, your parents may have taken responsibility for making sure you woke up and made it to school on time. Some of your teachers may have distributed study guides and prescribed exactly what you should do for homework. In order to be successful, you simply did as you were told.

In contrast, now that you are an adult in college you will have to take charge of managing your time and planning your homework. You have to set your alarm, take care of all of your personal needs, get to class on time, and be ready to learn. No one will make you do it, and no one will check to see what you do or don't do. If you don't get it right—if you don't make learning a personal priority—then you are likely to earn some failing grades.

Rarely do you hear college students use the term "homework." Instead you might hear them use the term "study," as in "I have to study this weekend for a history test on Tuesday." This is probably because college professors almost never assign homework. Generally speaking homework is a set of practice exercises assigned by a teacher; usually, it contributes to students' grades for the class. Unlike high school teachers, college professors leave it to students to decide for themselves how to go about learning the required information. So if college professors don't assign homework, does that mean you don't have to do work at home? No. It means that you will have to create your own reading, learning, and practice exercises, and assign them to yourself. That is the definition of studying.

Professors may not assign homework, but they definitely expect you to invest a lot of time and effort in studying. Students who practice good, regular study habits find it much easier to learn and earn high marks in college. Developing an effective study plan is one of the things that you will explore in this book.

In College, Studying Happens Outside of Class.

Another important thing that you need to know about college is that most studying—and therefore most learning—will happen outside of class. Typically, the bulk of learning in school prior to college occurs in the classroom. In college, you will have to do a lot of reading and studying before you even go to class in order to be successful at learning. The figures vary from course to course, but as a general rule, about two-thirds of the learning in college takes place outside of class.

Figure 1.1 illustrates the phenomenon that the higher you go in college, the more studying and learning will take place outside of class.

Figure 1.1 Venues for Studying and Learning at Various Academic Levels

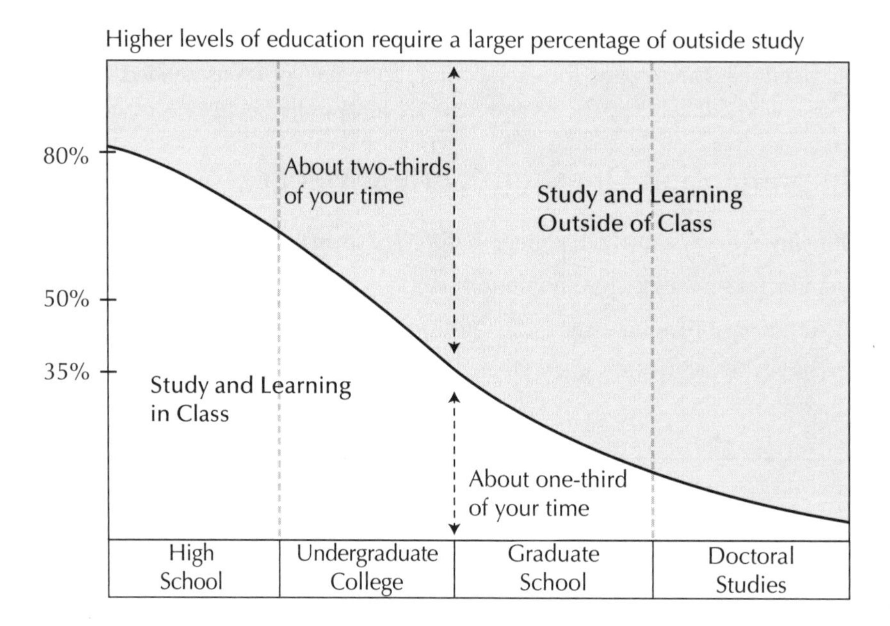

The College Board website offers the following sage advice: "All first-year college students contend with this bend in the learning curve, so don't think having to struggle to keep up is somehow a failing on your part. Give yourself an opportunity to adjust gradually to the new academic demands. Choose a course load that includes some challenging classes and others that will be less intense."[3]

It is not the case that every college course requires two hours of study outside of class for every hour of class time. Each course that you take in college will be somewhat different. Some will require you to spend a lot time studying outside of class, and others not so much. Taken together, however, the average is about two hours outside of class for every hour spent in class. In order to be successful, you will need to determine how much time you will need to spend studying for each of your classes, and plan that study time as a part of your daily routine. One thing that every college course has in common is a document called the *syllabus*.

The Syllabus Is Your Best Friend.

In college, the syllabus will be your best friend. The syllabus is the main way in which professors assist you in planning your study regimen. The syllabus is a document that is distributed, or otherwise made available (sometimes online), on the first day of classes. It contains lots of important and useful information about the expectations of the course and often includes descriptions of assignments, along with the deadlines for them, and the dates and content of exams. You need to know this information to be successful in the course. Make reading the syllabus a top priority, and ask your professor to clarify any part of the syllabus that you do not understand.

Apart from providing the syllabus, professors typically do not give homework or tell you how to study for their classes. *You* now have to decide for yourself when to study, how long to study, what to do when you study, and what information is important to study. You have to make up your own homework. This skill takes practice and time to learn. This book will help you get it right. Chapter 2 of this book will show you how to design a study regimen using your syllabus and a calendar so that you will be able to meet the deadlines you are given.

However, if classes have already begun you should not wait to read all your syllabi—you should read them carefully as soon as you have access to them. One of the things you should do right away is find out how you will be graded in each course, so that you can start keeping a record of your progress. The successful student never has to ask the professor, "How many days have I been absent?" or "What is my grade in this class so far?" A successful student will keep a personal record of absences and grades on exams or other assignments.

The assignment that accompanies this chapter (Assignment 1.1) will help you get started with the process of keeping a record of your grades. Assignment 1.1 provides you with a single page on which to record your progress. You will need a separate page for each course, so make copies as needed. As soon as you get a syllabus for each course, immediately use the Assignment 1.1 form to list the exams or other assignments that will be required. Later, when you receive grades on the exams or assignments, you can record them in the space provided. Any time you are absent from a class session, you should record the date of the absence in the space provided on the form. In this way you will always know where you stand in the course; and if some of your early grades are poor, you can take steps early in the semester to improve. Constant monitoring of your progress and early intervention are keys to success in college.

Want to learn more? Try these resources.

High School Versus College Life: A Freshman Year Guide to Different Student Academic Expectations, by Naomi Rockler-Gladen (Highly Recommended)
http://bvtlab.com/pUe77

How Is College Different from High School?
First-Year Experience Program website, Montgomery College
http://bvtlab.com/772A7

Montgomery College's *The First-Year Experience Program* website offers the following advice on transitioning to college[2]

Take control of your own education: think of yourself as a scholar.

Get to know your professors; they are your single greatest resource.

Be assertive. Create your own support systems, and seek help when you realize you may need it.

Take advantage of academic and student support services on campus.

Take control of your time. Plan ahead to satisfy academic obligations first, and then make room for everything else.

Stretch yourself: Enroll in at least one course that really challenges you.

Make thoughtful decisions: Don't take a course just to satisfy a requirement, and don't drop any course too quickly.

Think beyond the moment: Set goals for each semester [or quarter], the year, and your college career.

Making a smooth transition into college is the first step on the road to success in college.

Reading Comprehension Question 1.2 (Literal Comprehension)

Which of the following is one of the major differences between college and high school?

a. In college, two-thirds of learning takes place outside of class.

b. In college, professors are nurturing and directive.

c. In college, professors have all the answers.

d. In high school, teachers are not as highly directive as college professors.

1.3 The Road to Success

What Is Student Success?

This student success book is designed to orient the new college student to the unique challenges associated with college life. The overarching goals of the book are to enable the student to avoid the pitfalls that often result in failure and to seize the opportunities that lead to success. This book will help you to problem solve as you go through your first year of college.

What is success? You may find a plethora of statements defining success in books and on the Internet. For example, consider these somewhat humorous success statements from the online *Quote Garden* (http://bvtlab.com/78P76):

"I couldn't wait for success ... so I went ahead without it." Jonathan Winters

"Success is simply a matter of luck. Ask any failure." Earl Wilson

"Some people dream of success while others wake up and work hard at it." Winston Churchill

"It's not that I'm so smart; it's just that I stay with problems longer." Albert Einstein

"Don't be afraid to give your best to what seemingly are small jobs. Every time you conquer one, it makes you that much stronger. If you do the little jobs well, the big ones will tend to take care of themselves." Dale Carnegie

Some of these statements about success are funny and even insightful, but they only address the topic of success in a general sense. How do you define success specifically with regard to your experience in college? In Critical Thinking Activity 1.1, which appeared at the beginning of this chapter, you were asked to think about and write a definition of success in college. So—what is success in college? Success in college ultimately means graduating (i.e., earning a degree); it also includes all of the quality milestones along the way, such as learning as much as you can and maintaining a high grade point average (GPA). Success in college means not only becoming better certified but also better qualified.

So—What Is Success in College?

There is no question that one of the main purposes of attending college is to acquire a credential. The college diploma is meant to signify that the student has met certain academic and other requirements that have prepared them for any number of careers, generally, as well as careers associated with their discipline, specifically. The credential is supposed to represent a certain level of learning and mastery. Usually, the way that mastery is determined is through grades. If a student makes high marks or grades, it is assumed that they have learned what they need to know to master the discipline. However, it is important to distinguish between grades and learning—as they are not always the same.

In and of itself, a grade does not represent learning. For example, when students cram for an exam the night before a test and are able to score high enough on the test to pass the course—but literally forget 80 to 90 percent of what they studied within a short time thereafter—then those students will have acquired a passing grade but might not have really learned what they need to know. If too many of the grades they receive were acquired in this manner, then their diplomas are a misrepresentation of their actual learning. If passing without truly learning becomes ubiquitous at a particular college or university, then the status of a degree from that institution loses much of its value in the job market. In an extreme case, the diploma loses its meaning and is nothing but a piece of paper. Therefore, it's very important that as you are progressing through your academic program, you strive to make high grades through learning. If you truly learn the material, you will automatically make higher grades—and you will be prepared for the career of your choice. While you must take care to always make good grades, never lose your focus on learning. The real reason you are in college is to learn and change and grow—and to become a person worthy of your credentials.

Success Means Becoming Qualified

If you focus on learning rather than grades, you will become qualified. If you focus on grades to the exclusion of learning, you may become certified, but you won't be qualified. You will be a fraud. No student enters college planning to be a fraud. Sadly, the structure of our educational system—with its focus on grades and credentials—pushes students in that direction. The wise student will not succumb to the path of least resistance—he or she will not focus on grades alone to the exclusion of learning. Instead, the wise student will design study plans that give him or her time to actually learn the material, to grow and to change and in the process to attain high marks and a credential. In this way, the wise student will become both certified and highly qualified. The personal benefits of becoming both certified and qualified remain with you for years to come because you have been changed.

So the primary purpose of taking a course is not to simply pass the exam or get the credit—instead, the primary purpose is to learn something important. Every course that you take should change you in some way. Even though your beliefs, values, and personal goals may not change, your knowledge of the world, your ability to think critically, your ability to reason, and your ability to apply the sum of your knowledge to new challenges—all should be improved. Therefore, it is safe to say that a liberal arts education should change you. It should make you a better person. That is success.

What Is Failure in College?

Failure in college can manifest as flunking out, dropping out, or losing out. Flunking out happens when students accumulate too many failing grades and find it nearly impossible to raise their GPA to the level required for graduation. Dropping out occurs for many reasons. Sometimes students drop out due to factors beyond their control, but too many students drop out for academic reasons. Losing out is what happens when a student matriculates without being challenged, without changing for the better, and without preparing for what lies ahead. This book aims to help you avoid all of these types of failure.

1.4 Attitudes and Resources for Success

This book is designed to help students connect to the various resources, and to develop attitudes and habits, that will support their success. Table 1.2 illustrates these goals by listing some of the resources and attitudes that the book will address. As illustrated in the table, attitudes involve both perspectives (How do you view the task at hand?) and practices (How do you approach the task at hand?). Resources include knowledge (What things do you need to know to be successful?), tools (What tools will help you achieve success?), and helpers (Who is here to help me be successful?). Each of these items is very important.

Table 1.2 Examples of Attitudes and Resources for Success

ATTITUDES		RESOURCES		
Perspectives	**Practices**	**Knowledge**	**Tools**	**Helpers**
Focus on learning	Maintain a study calendar	College policies and procedures	Library resources	Academic advisors
Embrace responsibility	Develop a study plan for each class	Expectations in college	The college website	Tutors
View academics as a top priority	Develop and maintain a long-term graduation plan	How to develop and follow a study plan	College catalog	Faculty
Hold realistic expectations for college	Attend cultural events that enhance learning	How to design a long-term academic plan	Student organizations	College counselor
Commit time and effort to college success	Participate in student organizations	How to prepare for early registration	Fitness facilities	College staff in various departments
Eliminate hindrances to success	Develop a fitness plan	Principles of time management	Planning calendar	Campus security
	Develop positive relationships with helpers	How to listen and take notes	Written study plan	
	Assess yourself		This manual	
	Get help early			

Reading Comprehension Question 1.3 (Inferential Comprehension)

What is the main reason for this college success guide?

a. To enable the student to avoid the pitfalls that often result in failure and to seize the opportunities that lead to success

b. To keep track of new students in the system

c. To provide the students with an easy book for their first semester

d. None of the above

Reading Comprehension Question 1.4 (Analysis)

Why is it important for the student to know what happens in his or her first year of college?

a. Then the student can be prepared for classes.

b. Then the student can achieve the intended benefit from college.

c. Then the student will be clear about what is required in college.

d. All of the above

Summary

This chapter discussed the transition to college and contrasted the expectations and experiences of students in college compared to high school. You were challenged to create your own definition of success in college and were informed that college success involves the acquisition of both a credential (earning the degree) and a quality education (becoming a changed person through learning). There was also a brief discussion about attitudes and resources that will help you to be successful. We will explore specific attitudes and strategies in more detail in other chapters.

Review Questions

1.1

Instructions: Following are five true-false statements taken from the information in this chapter. First, try to answer them without looking back at the chapter. Then review the chapter to see how well you did.

Question & Answer	Rationale
Circle true or false for each of the following statements.	**Write an explanation stating why each statement is true or false.**
1. Tests are given more frequently in college than in high school. True or False	Your Rationale:
2. College is very similar to high school except that you live away from home and you have to study a little more. True or False	Your Rationale:
3. If you ask your professor to help you with time management, he or she will call you every morning to wake you up for class. True or False	Your Rationale:
4. Class meetings are very important in college because most learning occurs in class. True or False	Your Rationale:
5. The road to success involves your attitude toward learning, as well as your use of campus resources. True or False	Your Rationale:

Name: ____________________

Chapter One

Study Guide

Chapter 1, Goal 1: The student will be able to describe the ways in which high school and college are different.

Questions	Answers & Notes

Name: ______________________________

Chapter One **Study Guide**

Chapter 1, Goal 2: The student will be able to anticipate many of the challenges associated with attending college.

Questions	Answers & Notes

Name: ______________________________

Chapter One

Study Guide

Chapter 1, Goal 3: The student will be able to define success in college in terms of both certification and qualification.

Questions	Answers & Notes

Maintain a Record of Your Progress

Goal:

The purpose of this activity is to prepare the student to constantly monitor his or her grades for each course so that he or she will be able to remedy failing grades early in the semester.

Objective:

The student will keep a record of his or her grades for each course and will use the record to evaluate his or her progress on a regular basis.

Instructions:

The successful student never has to ask the professor, "How many days have I been absent?" or "What is my grade in this class so far?" because a successful student will keep his or her own record of absences and grades on exams or other assignments. You can use the **"Record of Grades and Attendance"** form provided on the next page of this textbook. You will need a separate copy of the form for each of your courses, so make photocopies of the form before you write on it.

Follow these steps:

Step 1: Consult the syllabus for each of your courses to determine how the semester grade will be calculated for that particular course. Use the form called **"Record of Grades and Attendance"** provided on the next page to list of all of the factors that contribute to the semester grade (i.e., exam scores, attendance, grades on essays, grades for discussions, and so on).

Step 2: Keep a record of the grades earned or points earned for each of these factors. Update it every time you receive a new grade or assignment feedback. If your grade is low or the feedback on other assignments suggest that you could do better, then think about ways that you can improve before the next graded assignment is due.

Recording your grades in one place will make it easier for you to monitor your progress throughout the semester. You will need to complete a separate record of grades for each of your courses. Recording your grades in one place will make it easier for you to monitor your progress throughout the semester.

Record of Grades and Attendance

Name: ______________________________ **Course:** ______________________________

What is the semester grade formula for this course? ______________________________

Exam or Assessment	Date Submitted	Grade/Score	Attendance Record
1.			You should attend every class. However, if you are ever absent from this class, record the date of the absence below so that you can keep track of them and calculate how they affect your grade.
2.			
3.			
4.			
5.			
6.			
7.			1.
8.			2.
9.			3.
10.			4.
11.			5.
12.			What is the attendance policy for this course?
13.			
14.			
15.			
Totals			

NOTES:

Chapter 2 Roadmap

Organizing: Plan Your Work and Then Work Your Plan

In this chapter you will learn how to create a study plan for each course that you are taking this semester. In order to create a written study plan, you will need to use a copy of the syllabus for each class you are taking along with the calendar and planning tools found in this chapter.

This chapter roadmap page presents the formal learning goals for this chapter and a check list that you should follow as you read and study the chapter.

Student Learning Goals for This Chapter

After completing this chapter the student should be able to do the following:

1. List six behaviors that rob the student of time for effective study and explain how each behavior could prevent the student from having a successful study regimen.
2. Describe and create an effective study plan using a semester (or other academic term) calendar, a weekly schedule, and checklist for individual study sessions.
3. List and describe the components of the Alphabet Approach to time management.

Checklist for This Chapter

Target date/ deadline	Check when completed	Activity
________	❑	1. Complete Critical Thinking Activity 2.1.
________	❑	2. Convert the learning goals above to questions that you can answer as you read the chapter. Write your questions on the study guide pages near the end of this chapter.
________	❑	3. Read the chapter.
________	❑	4. Try to answer the reading comprehension questions as you come to them in the chapter. Check each answer by comparing it to the list of correct answers in the back of the book. If any answer was not correct, then review the passages preceding the question to see why you missed the question.
________	❑	5. Use the study guide pages near the end of this chapter to write down the answers to the questions you created in Step 2 of this list. Once completed, these answered questions will be your study guide for the quiz.
________	❑	6. Write down any questions, insights, or comments that you have as you read so that you can bring them up in class (if applicable).
________	❑	7. Complete Review Questions 2.1.
________	❑	8. Complete Assignment 2.1 (Mark your monthly calendar).
________	❑	9. Complete Assignment 2.2 (Develop study plans).
________	❑	10. Complete Assignment 2.3 (Create a weekly study appointment sheet).
________	❑	11. Complete Assignment 2.4 (Create study session checklists).

CRITICAL THINKING ACTIVITY 2.1

"Failures don't plan to fail; they fail to plan."

—*Harvey MacKay*[1]

Use the space provided in this page to write your thoughts about this Harvey MacKay quote. What does the quote mean? Give an example to explain the quote. How does the quote apply to success in college?

Organizing:

Plan Your Work and Then Work Your Plan

2

"

Time is free, but it's priceless. You can't own it, but you can use it. You can't keep it, but you can spend it. Once you've lost it, you can never get it back.

Harvey MacKay[2]

I gotta work out. I keep saying it all the time. I keep saying I gotta start working out. It's been about two months since I've worked out. And I just don't have the time. Which uh ... is odd. Because I have the time to go out to dinner. And uh ... and watch TV. And get a bone density test. And uh ... try to figure out what my phone number spells in words ...

Ellen DeGeneres[1]

"

Getting organized when you enter college is one of the most important things you can do to ensure your success. In college, you will quickly find that time is a valuable commodity—and you need to it use wisely. It is often the case that college professors use the first class to discuss their expectations for the course. They also provide a written document, the syllabus, that details these expectations. Sometimes, if the first day of class is taken up by introductions and a discussion of expectations alone, new students get the incorrect idea that they don't have to do anything until the next class. Nothing is further from the truth, however. What you need to do is take the information that the professor has given you and use it to plan how you will approach the course for the entire semester. Your plan should include practical information—such as the dates of exams—as well as descriptions of the expected content on exams and the nature of other assignments (e.g., papers or presentations). In this chapter, you will learn how to deal with time constraints and to create an effective study plan for a college course.

One of the differences between high school and college (Chapter 1) regarded time management. In high school, it's likely that your teachers and parents constantly reminded you of timelines and due dates on assignments. In contrast, as a college student it is your responsibility to set your own schedule and manage your time.

The successful student has a plan for how he or she will fit studying into a daily schedule that is already full of responsibilities. To be successful as a student, you will need to purposefully plan time for your studies, rather than just expect yourself to "fit it in" as you go along. The challenges of gaining an education demand that you value your time highly—and the same goes for those whom you love. Going to college is a major life decision—one that should be made with an understanding that you must make space in your life for school. It is not an "add-on" that you can just plunk into your schedule for a few hours a week, hoping you will "get through it."

To be successful, you will need to treat school as the serious obligation that it is; one that requires time, money, and other important resources. Having said that, college is also an exciting and challenging time during which you will grow and learn in amazing ways.

Good time management is a tool that can help you succeed in this new life endeavor. The successful student knows that time is a commodity that must be controlled and that it should be used in specific, predefined ways. If you are able to determine how to spend your time, (i.e., how much time should be spent studying) and turn those findings into a smart, user-friendly study guide, then you have already come a long way down the path to success in college.

This chapter is about time management, specifically as it relates to the needs of college students. First, you will learn about time management in general, including some tips on balancing your time. Then you will learn step-by-step how to develop your own successful study plan. Also in this chapter, you will learn how to use your syllabus and a calendar to design a study regimen that will enable you to learn what you need by the deadlines that you have been given.

2.1 Time Management: A Myth

There is no such thing as time management. Time itself cannot be manipulated or controlled (outside of science fiction). No matter how hard you try, you cannot add a single second to the day. It is not time that can be managed, but rather how one uses time that can be controlled. How efficiently do you use time? Knowing how to use your time well is vital when it comes to success in college. In college, you will probably spend around fifteen hours a week in classes; but much more time will be needed to read, study, think, and learn everything that you need to be successful in those classes. It takes time to be successful in college. There simply is no shortcut.

Reading Comprehension Question 2.1 (Knowledge)

Which of the following is true of time management?

a. You can manipulate the time you have for studying.
b. You can't manage your time, but you can control how you use it.
c. You will find that time management is usually not helpful in college.
d. You will discover that time itself can actually be controlled.

A. Time Pirates

Pirates were thieves who roamed the seas to rob unsuspecting mariners of their treasures. When you were in high school, you might have noticed that you were—and perhaps still are—susceptible to certain behaviors and other factors that robbed you of time. You may be unaware of other factors or behaviors that nevertheless have the same effect. The roll call of these pirates includes procrastination, distractions, use of cell phones, use of excessive alcohol or drugs, use of shortcuts when studying, and feeling that you must be nice to all at the expense of your own top priorities. Some of these pirates even come disguised as time-savers. In truth, these pirates are an even bigger problem in college because they are compounded by the stress of being a first-time college student. So it is more important than ever to recognize them, get the jump on them, and take measures to prevent them.

Procrastination is when you put off doing something until a later date or time. Usually people use procrastination because they find the task to be unpleasant—a chore—or they really just don't want to do it. They let themselves off the hook mentally by thinking, "I can do it later." One problem with this behavior is that sometimes "later" never comes; sometimes the task never gets done. Another problem is that sometimes the task gets done, but it gets done poorly because it was put off until the last minute. For example, if you wait until the last few days before a paper is due to begin writing the paper, you will forfeit the opportunity for revision; thus, the quality of your work will suffer. The end result is a lower grade. Finally, procrastination sometimes has the deleterious effect of making you more stressed and making you feel guilty. Therefore, procrastination is a time pirate because it steals the time that you needed to produce quality work and feel good about it. Most of us have been robbed by procrastination at one time or another—just don't let it steal your college success.

Distractions can take the form of environmental factors that keep you from doing what you need to do, such as a roommate's loud music or the neighbor's barking dog. In such cases, you may need to change your environment or find a better place or time to study. Other lower priority tasks, such as doing laundry, can also be a distraction from studying. This is why it is important to include the basics of daily living in your time management plan. If you know that you have a special time set aside for laundry and a different time set aside for studying, then you don't have to deal with the psychological stress of worrying that perhaps you should be studying while you are doing laundry and vice versa.

The **cell phone** can be a wonderful tool and even a time-saver. However, for some students, the phone becomes a proverbial "ball and chain" because anticipating the next text message prevents them from paying attention in class or fully concentrating when they study. The cell phone does not steal your study time—it kills your study time (by rendering it ineffective) and in so doing kills your grades, making it the worst type of time pirate.

Many students incorrectly assume that their multi-tasking skills will enable them to keep up with text messages on their phone while listening to a college lecture. That is a myth. In reality, if you are texting (or reading a text) during a class session, you will not gain the full benefit of that lecture or discussion—and if you are called on, you will likely appear dumfounded and out of it because you haven't really kept up with what was going on in class. If you can't resist playing with your phone, then it would be better for you to turn it off and put it away during class or study sessions. Don't let the cell phone steal your success.

I often recommend that my students take a few minutes before each of their classes to use their cell phones (perhaps to check email, Facebook, Twitter, or some other social account, and to send any urgent messages). Then put the phone away for the entire duration of class and check the phone again as soon as class is over. Even if you have classes back to back, you usually have time to check your phone if it's truly important. Since most college classes last only about an hour, the check-before-and-after system works pretty well for most students.

Another time pirate that kills your grades is a **belief in shortcuts for studying**. You will not perform well on college level exams if you employ a shallow learning approach (e.g., trying to memorize all of the bolded words in the textbook rather than building an understanding of the concepts that are presented) because you think that is a way to study faster. Such so-called shortcuts may save you time, but they will kill your grades because a meaningful percentage of a college-level exams will extend beyond merely defining terms—instead requiring you to understand and apply the concepts.

One of the most common misconceptions, which many students perceive as a shortcut, is the idea that you can cram for an exam the night before. "Cramming" is the practice of not reading or studying anything for weeks and then trying to do it all the night before the exam. If it is the night before an exam and you haven't studied for a while, then cramming may be your one and only option. But if, long before the exam date, you think to yourself: "I don't need to study every night because I will just cram before the test instead (as a shortcut)," then you have incorrectly assumed that cramming will be enough to make you successful. The truth is that you will earn higher grades and find college much more pleasant (and less stressful) if you study a little each day rather than counting on cramming to save the day. So plan out your study time at the beginning of the semester and commit to your plan, and you will have much greater success.

Aside from the health dangers associated with **excessive drinking and drug use**, any time you spend in a compromised mental state due to the abuse of any substance is definitely not time that can be used to study effectively. Therefore, when your drinking or drug use extends into the time that you have reserved for studying—or if its aftereffects (i.e., a hangover) compromise your study time—you have been robbed by a time pirate.

Finally, **trying to be nice at the expense of your top priorities** can cause you to use your time poorly. Being successful means that you will have to say "no" on occasion to invitations, opportunities, or pleas that take you away from your study schedule. The desires of others, when put above your own needs, can steal your study time. Just say "no" if you know that saying "yes" will prevent you from necessary studying.

Reading Comprehension Question 2.2 (Literal Comprehension)

Which of the following are time pirates in college?

a. Procrastination
b. Distractions
c. Use of cell phones
d. Drinking excessively
e. All of the above

B. How Much Time Do I Have, Anyway?

In order to "manage" your time, you must have an idea of how much time you have available to manage. The first step in time management is to assess your own, unique, personal schedule. You can do this by estimating the time you spend on certain activities; or if you are unsure, you can write down when, and for how long, you do various things over the course of a week to see where your time goes. It may be helpful for you to keep a log for your first few weeks of college. Keeping a log is much more accurate than trying to "guesstimate" the time you spend. Although keeping a log requires some effort, you will find that time spent analyzing your schedule can be worth its weight in gold.

C. How Much Time Do I Have for Studying?

With regard to success in college, the pertinent question will be "How much time do I have for studying?" As part of the study plan described in this chapter, you will use a weekly planner to map out when you will be in classes, at work, and fulfilling other obligations. Then you can look at the remaining blank time slots to decide when you will study for each of your classes. This simple procedure will give you an idea of how many hours you have left for studying and when those hours are during the day or week. So how do you become more efficient? How can you use the time that you have to maximize your success? This is where a well-designed study plan helps you succeed.

D. Plan Your Work; Then Work Your Plan!

Effective time management involves getting organized, setting goals, understanding what is required to achieve your goals, establishing priorities, planning activities, avoiding distractions, staying on track, maintaining balance, and following through with your plan. It is as simple as this: you must plan your work and then work your plan.

Many students know how to get organized but never make the effort to do it. Just do it. There are many books, tapes, videos, and websites that detail various organizational approaches. Certainly a person might resonate more with one type of plan than another. However, for the purpose of this book, a simple, specific and detailed plan that targets your needs as a college student will be outlined.

2.2 The Study Plan

Every student needs to have some sort of planner—whether it is a paper-and-pencil planner, an online planner, or some other sort of electronic planner. A planner should include a calendar and should allow you to keep track of meetings, events, and commitments; to schedule tasks and activities that support your goals; and to flag items for priority. This book will discuss how to use a planner, how to develop a plan for studying, and how to break down your study plan into manageable parts.

If you don't use a planner already, it would be a good idea to get one that you like. Paper-and-pencil planners are usually for a one-year period and are divided into either months or weeks. You can even get planners specifically for the academic year, which are sometimes helpful in college; these are most readily available at your college bookstore. It would be preferable to get a planner that has each week outlined with hours for each day. That way you can write out a detailed schedule including specific times for each activity.

This book will describe the steps you can follow to create your study plan using a paper calendar/planner to illustrate the process. Even if you prefer to use an electronic planner instead of a paper calendar, you should still find it easy to apply ideas from this chapter. However, you will probably need to use paper worksheets or paper calendar pages to figure out the details of your own schedule before you record it electronically.

Paper calendar booklets are available at very low cost. A worksheet and some blank calendar template pages are provided at the end of this chapter along with the assignment pages. Make copies for yourself as needed. (Always save one blank version of each template in this book, for making future copies if the need arises.)

You will need to design a study plan that is consistent with the academic term used at your college. An academic term is the period of time between the first day of classes and either the last day of classes or the end of final exams (which usually occur the week after the last day of classes). Many colleges operate on a semester system in which the college year includes two 15–16 week semesters (usually called fall semester and spring semester). There may also be opportunities to take classes during one or more shorter summer semesters. Other colleges use a quarter system in which there are four 10–11 week terms called quarters with short breaks between each one. Still other colleges have scheduling arrangements different from the semester or the quarter systems. You should simply tailor your study plan to match whichever scheduling arrangement your college uses. For the sake of simplicity, throughout this book we will use the term "semester" to refer generically to the academic term. Keep in mind, however, that your study plans should be built around whatever system is used at your particular college.

Components of the Study Plan

It is a good idea to design a study plan with three levels using three tools:

1. A plan for the semester (using a monthly calendar)
2. A plan for each week (using a week-at-a-glance appointment page)
3. A plan for each study session (using a study session ticket)

Once you have figured out an overall plan of action (which will be described in the next few pages), you should reserve a few minutes every week to review your progress within your plan and to make adjustments.

Your plan needs to be **written** (not just remembered in your head), **specific**, and **detailed.** Then you can look at it, think about it, follow it, make adjustments to it (by rescheduling tasks anytime you see that you have failed to follow it), and use it as a guide to help you keep your priorities straight. Remember, a good study plan must include not only **when** and **how long** you plan to study but also **exactly what study activities you will do** during the scheduled study time. Table 2.1 details each part of the study plan.

Creating Your Study Plan Tools

Now, let's go through each of the components of the study plan outlined in Table 2.1. The following text, together with Assignments 2.1, 2.2, and 2.3 (found at the end of this chapter), will guide you as you create your own personal study plan tools.

Table 2.1 Study Tools

The Tool	Organize	Write Down
SEMESTER CALENDAR (Use the appropriate weeks on a monthly calendar.)	DUE DATES Make a note of when things are due and any college-related deadlines that affect you.	Due dates for all assignments Dates of exams College deadlines Relevant college events
WEEKLY APPOINTMENT PAGE	WHEN YOU WILL STUDY and FOR HOW LONG Keep track of when you will be in class, and when you will study outside of class.	Separately for each course you will write the following: When class meets Exactly when during the week you will study for the class
STUDY SESSION TICKET	WHAT YOU WILL DO (when you study) and HOW YOU WILL DO IT	For each study session, write the following: What will you read? (include page numbers) What will you write? What other learning strategies will you use? What learning activities will you do during that study session?

Tool 1: The Monthly Calendar

Start with the big picture. For this you will need a monthly calendar or a semester-at-a-glance calendar. These two options are illustrated in Figure 2.1.

Some students like to use a calendar that has all of the dates for the entire semester on a single page. A semester-at-a-glance calendar page can help you to get a good feel for how the deadlines and exams are spaced out over the term. Some colleges provide copies through a student resources center or on the college website, but if you prefer the semester-at-a-glance format and your college does not provide one, then you can always create your own. Otherwise, you can simply use any monthly calendar. The advantage of the monthly calendar is that you can record more information for any single date. A few blank calendar template pages are provided for you at the end of this chapter. You can make copies of those and use them to create your own calendars, if you wish.

Some students already keep all of their appointments and deadlines on a computer, an electronic tablet, or a cell phone. That is fine if it meets your academic needs. However, you may find that for your very first year of college, a paper-and-pencil calendar will be more helpful to you. Whichever type of calendar you choose, just be sure it is the one you are most comfortable with and that you will be able to use it to keep up with your studies.

Assignment 2.1 guides you through the steps of marking your monthly or semester calendar. Before you start, you will need to obtain a copy of the official college calendar (usually found on the college website) and a syllabus for each of your classes. Then you will be ready to copy all of the important events from each of these documents onto your semester or monthly calendar (see Figure 2.1). Some students find it helpful to use a different color to highlight the items associated with different classes.

When you mark your calendar, remember to include the following items (when applicable):

- The dates for all of your quizzes or exams
- The due dates for all of your assignments (e.g., papers or projects)
- The dates for administrative deadlines (e.g., the last day to withdraw without academic penalty, the fee deadlines, the graduation application deadlines, and the date midterm grades will be posted)
- The dates and times of your final exams (some college finals may be given on a different day and time than your normal class session)
- The dates of campus events that you may wish to attend

Figure 2.1 Record Assignments and Deadlines on the Monthly Calendar

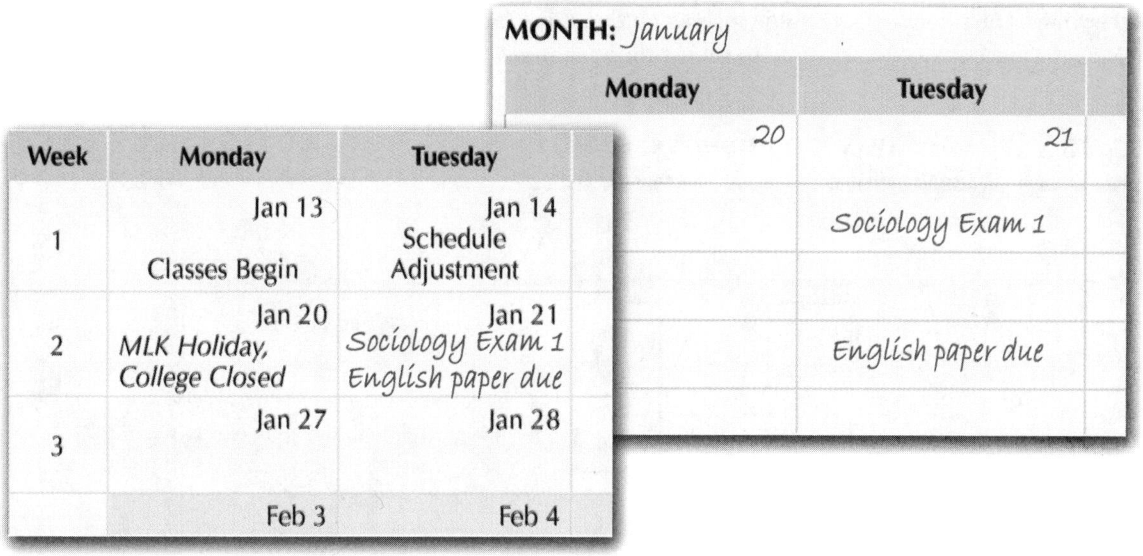

MONTH: January

Monday	Tuesday
20	21
	Sociology Exam 1
	English paper due

Week	Monday	Tuesday
1	Jan 13 Classes Begin	Jan 14 Schedule Adjustment
2	Jan 20 *MLK Holiday, College Closed*	Jan 21 Sociology Exam 1 English paper due
3	Jan 27	Jan 28
	Feb 3	Feb 4

Tool 2: The Weekly Appointment Calendar

The second tool you will need for your personal study plan is a weekly appointment calendar page. This is simply a page that allows you to block off appointments for different times during each day and to see the appointments for one entire week on a single page.

In order to create this tool, you will need some of the same materials that you used to mark your monthly calendar. These include a copy of the syllabus for each of your courses, a copy of each course schedule (usually found in the syllabus), and the dates of events that you wish to attend (such as club meetings).

You can use the weekly appointment page as part of your study plan by blocking off and labeling the times that you have classes and the times that you plan to study for each course. Class attendance and study time are the top priorities of successful college students. The idea is that you are making an appointment with yourself to attend class and to study because you expect to do those things at the same time every week during the semester. You should also follow this procedure for other aspects of your weekly routine that are recurrent. Assignment 2.2 provides a worksheet that will help you plan when you will study for each course. Assignment 2.3 will guide you in the actual process of creating a weekly appointment page. A blank weekly appointment page is included for you to copy and use. Since step-by-step instructions are given with the assignment pages, there is no need to repeat them here.

Take a look at your schedule, and decide when the best times would be to study for each class. When you block out a period of time on your appointment calendar for studying, don't just give it a generic label it such as "study." Instead, label it very specifically, such as "Study Calculus" or "Study English Lit." You want to make sure that you plan enough study appointments to meet each course's study demands.

When planning how much study time to devote to a particular course, take into consideration what study activities are associated with that course and estimate how much time it will take you to complete those activities. (Some courses may require reading a book while others may require attempting to solve example problems.) *Remember: About two-thirds of the time you spend on studying and learning will be outside of class.* If you find that you need less time or more time for a particular course as the semester progresses, you can adjust your schedule for subsequent weeks. You should reserve a few minutes every week to review your progress regarding your plan and to make adjustments.

Once you have created one weekly appointment sheet that shows all of your consistently recurring commitments (including classes and study times), you can use it as a template that can be copied and filled in with the obligations particular to a given week. You should make enough copies of your template so that you have one for each of the weeks in the semester. Then, week by week, you can schedule other events for any of the times that are not already committed to class or study.

Since you have finished with your weekly appointment calendar (Figure 2.2), your firm obligations are already blocked off for each week and day; the remaining blank spaces now represent time slots that you have open for leisure activities or appointments that come up each week. If a major change occurs that alters your normal weekly schedule (such as getting a job in the middle of the semester), you will need to revise your master weekly schedule to reflect those changes.

Figure 2.2 Weekly Appointment Calendar

DATE → TIME ↓	Monday	Tuesday	Wednesday	Thursday	Friday	Saturday	Sunday
8 a.m.	Math class		Math class				
9 a.m.			Study Math		Study Math		
10 a.m.							

What if something important comes up that you need to do during a time slot that you had reserved for studying? You can of course cancel your study appointment with yourself to attend to something urgent or important—so long as you reschedule the canceled study session.

Never cancel study time unless you reschedule it. Why? Because if you have done a good job of estimating the study demands of a particular course, reducing the time that you had planned may keep you from earning a good grade. For example, suppose Penny had scheduled ten hours of reading and study (on ten different days) between history exams. However, she canceled two of those study hours to get her hair done before an important job-related photo shoot, and she did not reschedule the two study hours. When she took the next history exam, she found that she was only able to answer about 75 percent of the exam questions correctly. She could have earned an A+, but she was only able to earn a C because of the loss of those two hours of reading and studying. Cancelling a study session so that she could get her hair done was not the problem—the problem was that she did not reschedule her planned and necessary study time.

You may find it useful to also block out time for the basics of daily living in your weekly appointment calendar—but as a matter of priority, try to schedule them around your study commitments and not the other way around. As stated elsewhere in this chapter, if you know that you have a special time set aside for laundry and a different time set aside for studying, then you don't have to deal with the psychological stress of worrying that perhaps you should be studying while you are doing laundry and vice versa.

Remember that the time you spend mapping out your detailed schedule for the entire semester is time well spent. This is how you create an environment for yourself in which you can be successful! It is similar to creating a financial budget—sometimes it feels tedious, but in the end it's worth it.

Tool 3: The Study Session Ticket

The information needed to complete the next assignment, the creation of a task list for each study session (or your "ticket" to study), can be found in the forms you completed for Assignment 2.2.

In order to be successful in college, *you need to plan each study session.* It is not good enough to simply mark the date and time that you plan to study on the calendar; you *must also make a checklist of exactly what you plan to do during the study session.* We call this your "study session ticket" because it will provide the information you need to complete a particular study session and because you can cut them out and use these tickets as bookmarks or markers in your calendar to keep up with exactly how and what you need to study for that week. This keeps your schedule and your study plan in the forefront of your mind, which is what you want in college.

You may need to create different types of study session tickets for different types of classes. For example, the study activities that you would do to prepare for a history class may be very different from the study activities that you would do to prepare for a math class.

A blank study session ticket template is provided with Assignment 2.4. You can make copies of the template and adapt it for each course. Then make as many of the adapted copies as you need. You will need one for each study session. Examples of things that you may wish to include on the study session ticket are: "read pages 324–425," "review notes," "define new vocabulary," and "record questions to ask in class." (See Figure 2.3 for an example of a completed study session ticket.)

The appropriate study activities will be different for each course. *Just make sure that you include enough detail to assess your own progress and to determine whether you are studying enough.* As you can see, Sharon Cooper (Figure 2.4) has set aside six hours of studying for approximately three hours of class per week. She is following the "two hours outside of class for every one hour inside class" formula. She will need to monitor her progress to determine whether or not this formula works for her. She might need to either reduce her study time or increase it, depending on her success in the course. The important thing is that she makes time to *evaluate* how she is doing with her study plan overall. You will need some time to reflect on your studying, classes, activities, and choices—perhaps after you have spent two to three weeks on campus. The ability to evaluate your progress is an important skill for success in college.

Once you have some experience putting study plans into action, you might find that it is more efficient to complete two to four weeks of study plans at a time. In other words, you may not want to map out the entire semester of study session tickets for all your courses in one sitting. That's fine. Just be sure to plan time to complete your tickets for each course in the remaining weeks of the semester, and don't procrastinate!

Figure 2.3 Example of a Completed Study Session Ticket

EXAMPLE: Study Session Ticket

Name: *Sharon Cooper*

Course: *Theoretical Physics*

Date: *9/12* **Time:** *10–11 a.m.*

- ☑ 1. *Check online for announcements*
- ☑ 2. *Review updated class notes*
- ☑ 3. *Review Ch. 2 Learning goals*
- ☑ 4. *Read Ch. 2, pp. 64–78*
- ☑ 5. *Check course online for professor's blog & mail*
- ☑ 6. *Make flashcards for Ch. 2*
- ☐ 7.
- ☐ 8.
- ☐ 9.
- ☐ 10.

Questions to ask in class:

Ask professor to explain the difference between protons and electrons when they are in zero gravity.

Note: *Had to quit early and didn't finish goals, so I need to add an extra 30 minutes and 6 more pages to the next session to catch up.*

2.3 The Alphabet Approach

Now that you have developed a serious study plan, you will be required to make a lot of time management decisions. Following is a simple technique that you may find helpful.

Nist and Holschuh discuss time management using what they call the "Alphabet Approach."[3] Specifically, they recommend the following four practices:

A = Anticipate and plan,
B = Break tasks down,
C = Cross things off, and
D = Don't procrastinate.

Figure 2.4 Example of a Completed Worksheet

Assignment 2.2
Study Time Management Worksheet for a Single Course

Student Name:	*Sharon Cooper*	Course:	*Theoretical Physics 231*
Date:	*August 19, 2015*	Credit Hours:	

Meeting Days and Times for the Course: *M, W, F; 8:30–9:45*

Details of the Study Plan:

WHEN will you study?

What Days?	*What Times?*		*How Long?*	
	Start	Finish		
Monday	*10:00 a.m.*	*11:00 a.m.*	*1 hour*	*minutes*
Tuesday	*10:00 a.m.*	*11:00 a.m.*	*1 hour*	*minutes*
Wednesday	*10:00 a.m.*	*11:00 a.m.*	*1 hour*	*minutes*
Thursday	*10:00 a.m.*	*11:00 a.m.*	*1 hour*	*minutes*
Friday	*10:00 a.m.*	*11:00 a.m.*	*1 hour*	*minutes*
Saturday	*10:00 a.m.*	*11:00 a.m.*	*1 hour*	*minutes*
Sunday				*minutes*
Weekly Total (Study Hours):			*6 hours*	*minutes*

WHAT study strategies will you use? (List what you will do.)

1. *Make flash cards.*
2. *Recopy notes in my own words.*
3. *Do the exercises at the end of each chapter.*
4. *Check to see if a study group is meeting.*
5. *Highlight important parts of the textbook and take notes when reading.*
6.

OTHER Notes or Information about this course:

Teaching Assistants (TA's) are available M, W, F 10–11 a.m.

Hollis Hall, Room 203; 555-123-1234; teachphysics@mycollege.edu

A = Anticipate and Plan

Once you have your class schedule for the term set, you can begin to map out your study time using the procedures already described in this chapter. The basic idea of having a concrete plan is that you will be able to anticipate your study needs and address them more effectively.

B = Break Tasks Down

Some learning activities or assignments must be done in stages over time, rather than on any particular day. An example of such an assignment would be writing a research paper. You cannot write it all in one study session. Instead, you must break the large task of the research paper into smaller parts (such as selecting a topic, finding information about the topic in the library, taking notes on the information, outlining the paper, writing a rough draft, revising and improving the draft, and finally printing the final draft). Plan times for each of the parts (usually on different days), and schedule the entire project in such a way that you will meet the deadline.

Creating tickets for each study session is another way to "break tasks down." The large task may be "study for history class," but that directive alone is too vague. So you make a list of the things you plan to actually *do* when you study for history class (for example, plan to read the chapter, outline the chapter, read your notes from class, make flashcards, answer questions assigned by the professor, and so on). You may also break down the study demands for a particular course by selecting a certain number of pages to read each day, rather than trying to tackle a lengthy reading assignment all at once. To determine how many pages to read each day, simply divide the total number of pages you have to read by the number of study sessions that you have planned before the date of the exam or the date on which the reading assignment is due. For example, if you have an exam coming up in two weeks covering one hundred pages of material and you have scheduled ten study sessions between now and the exam date, you will need to read and study ten pages during each study session.

C = Cross Things Off

As you work your way through your week, you will find that there is a certain sense of accomplishment gained from crossing things off your list. For some students, lists are also a great way to mitigate stress. Be sure to cross out any activities that you have completed. If you find that lists help you, you may want to eventually have short-term as well as long-term goals in list form. That way you can keep track of the small steps you are taking in order to reach a larger goal.

D = Don't Procrastinate

There are many reasons people procrastinate, including a fear of being wrong, a need to be perfect, a fear of limitations, or a feeling that you are facing an overwhelming task.[4] If you find that you really struggle with putting things off until the last minute, you may want to explore this topic in more depth than we have time for here. Many books have been written on procrastination. Consider the following techniques in your efforts to avoid it:

- Set reasonable goals
- Plan regularly
- Break tasks down into smaller parts
- Make and use "To Do" lists
- Post monthly and yearly calendars at home
- Force yourself to get started on a task even if you do not feel like it
- Ask for help
- Give yourself permission to be less than perfect
- Remember to schedule relaxation time ("down time") for yourself
- Reward yourself for tasks completed

Want to learn more?

Try these resources.

Are you a procrastinator?
This website provides some definitions and also some helpful hints:
http://bvtlab.com/77Y98

This academic website is devoted to helping students analyze and address procrastination:
http://bvtlab.com/3rg88

Reading Comprehension Question 2.3 (Inferential Comprehension)

Nist and Holschuh discuss time management using what they call the "Alphabet Approach." Specifically, they recommend which of the following practices?

a. Anticipate and plan, break tasks down, cross things off, and don't procrastinate.

b. Ask for help, reward yourself, do not be a perfectionist, and space out your work.

c. Set goals, plan regularly, use "to do" lists, and post a calendar.

d. All of the above

Summary

This chapter has addressed some basic principles that will help you manage your time effectively. You learned how important it is to design a personal study plan. Individual plans may vary, somewhat, for different personalities and different courses; however, a good plan is one that is 1) written, 2) detailed, and 3) specific.

In order to apply what you have learned in this chapter, you will need to organize your schedule using three tools: 1) the semester-at-a-glance or the monthly calendar, 2) the weekly appointment calendar, and 3) the individual study session ticket. Your plan should identify your goals; make provisions for the activities that are required to achieve your goals; support your top priorities; and allow you to maintain a healthy balance between work, study, and recreation. No plan can be successful unless you follow it, so **plan your work and then work your plan!**

Reading Comprehension Question 2.4 (Analysis)

Why is time management so important for student success?

a. Time is something many students have never learned to manage appropriately.

b. Time can be controlled and manipulated.

c. Time: the more you have, the more studying you can do.

d. Time is elusive, and there is never enough time to do what you need to do.

REVIEW QUESTIONS 2.1

Instructions: Following are five true-false statements taken from the information in this chapter. First, try to answer them without looking back at the chapter. Then review the chapter to see how well you did.

Question & Answer	Rationale
Circle true or false for each of the following statements.	**Write an explanation stating why each statement is true or false.**
1. Using the Alphabet Approach to scheduling involves techniques that begin with each letter of the alphabet, A to Z. **True or False**	Your Rationale:
2. Procrastination is a classic time pirate because it eats away at your time while you do nothing toward accomplishing the goal at hand. **True or False**	Your Rationale:
3. A good study plan must include not only when and how long you plan to study but also exactly what study activities you will do during the scheduled study time. **True or False**	Your Rationale:
4. The book explains how you can create your own academic planner. **True or False**	Your Rationale:
5. Research shows that in recent years college students have developed multi-tasking skills that enable them to keep up with text messages on their cell phones while effectively listening to a college lecture. **True or False**	Your Rationale:

Name: ______________________________

Chapter Two

Study Guide

Chapter 2, Goal 1: The student will be able to list six behaviors that rob the student of time for effective study and explain how each behavior could prevent the student from having a successful study regimen.

Questions	Answers & Notes

Name: ______________________________

Chapter Two

Study Guide

Chapter 2, Goal 2: The student will be able to describe and create an effective study plan using a semester calendar, a weekly schedule, and a checklist for individual study sessions.

Questions	Answers & Notes

Name: ______________________________

Chapter Two

Study Guide

Chapter 2, Goal 3: The student will be able to list and describe the components of the Alphabet Approach to time management.

Questions	Answers & Notes

Name: ____________________

Preparing for Class:
Use This Page to Record Questions or Insights to Discuss in Class.

Assignment 2.1

Mark Your Monthly Calendar

Goal:

The purpose of this activity is to enable the student to create an organized record of deadlines and other responsibilities in a monthly planner.

Objective:

The student will record deadlines, due dates, and other academic responsibilities on an appropriate monthly calendar, as described in Chapter 2.

Instructions:

A calendar planner is a very important tool for any student who wishes to be successful in college. You should use one to remind yourself of important deadlines and events and to keep yourself on track with a regular study regimen for each of the courses that you are taking. For this assignment you will simply record all of the important information about your courses on calendar pages.

Step 1: Gather the materials that you will need to complete this lab assignment. These include the following:

- A monthly calendar
- A copy of the syllabus for each of your courses
- A copy of your course schedule (usually found in the syllabus)
- A copy of the official college calendar (you can usually view it online)
- A list of dates and times for events that you wish to attend (such as club meetings)

Step 2: Review the materials you gathered for Step 1 to find all of the deadlines and other important dates you will need to remember. Record each of these deadlines or meeting dates in your monthly calendar.

Example Semester-at-a-Glance Calendar: Spring 2014

Week	Monday	Tuesday	Wednesday	Thursday	Friday
1	Jan 13 Classes Begin	Jan 14 Schedule Adjustment	Jan 15 Schedule Adjustment	Jan 16	Jan 17
2	Jan 20 *MLK Holiday, College Closed*	Jan 21	Jan 22	Jan 23 Fee Deadline	Jan 24
3	Jan 27	Jan 28	Jan 29	Jan 30	Jan 31
4	Feb 3	Feb 4	Feb 5	Feb 6	Feb 7
5	Feb 10	Feb 11	Feb 12	Feb 13	Feb 14 End of 5th week of classes
6	Feb 17 Midterm grades reported: Registrar	Feb 18	Feb 19	Feb 20	Feb 21
7	Feb 24	Feb 25	Feb 26	Feb 27	Feb 28
8	Mar 3	Mar 4	Mar 5 **Last day to withdraw w/o penalty**	Mar 6	Mar 7
9	Mar 10	Mar 11	Mar 12	Mar 13	Mar 14
10	Mar 17 *Spring Break*	Mar 18 *Spring Break*	Mar 19 *Spring Break*	Mar 20 *Spring Break*	Mar 21 *Spring Break*
11	Mar 24	Mar 25	Mar 26	Mar 27	Mar 28
12	Mar 31	Apr 1	Apr 2	Apr 3	Apr 4
13	Apr 7	Apr 8	Apr 9	Apr 10	Apr 11
14	Apr 14	Apr 15	Apr 16	Apr 17	Apr 18
15	Apr 21	Apr 22	Apr 23	Apr 24 7–8 pm Honors Program	Apr 25
16	Apr 28	Apr 29	Apr 30	May 1	May 2 Classes End
17	May 5 Finals Week May 5–8	May 6	May 7	May 8	May 9 Graduation

Note: A blank semester-at-a-glance calendar, a blank two-page per month calendar, and a blank one-page per month calendar appear on the following pages.

Week	Monday	Tuesday	Wednesday	Thursday	Friday
1					
2					
3					
4					
5					
6					
7					
8					
9					
10					
11					
12					
13					
14					
15					
16					
17					

MONTH:

Monday	Tuesday	Wednesday	Thursday

Friday	Saturday	Sunday	NOTES

MONTH:			Plan Your Work and Then Work Your Plan			
Monday	Tuesday	Wednesday	Thursday	Friday	Saturday	Sunday

Assignment 2.2

Develop Study Plans for Courses

Goal:

The purpose of this activity is to help the student to create a written study plan for each course.

Objective:

The student will create a specific, detailed study plan for each course.

Instructions:

For this assignment you must write a brief description of your study plan for each of the courses you are taking this semester. Use the form called **Study Time Management Worksheet for a Single Course**.

Follow these steps:

Step 1: Prepare the proper number of forms.

Earlier in the chapter (Figure 2.3) is an example of a completed **Study Time Management Worksheet for a Single Course**. Following are four blank copies of the form. You will need one for each of your courses. Therefore, please make copies of the form as needed and always keep one blank copy on hand for future courses. For example, if you find that this exercise really helps you, then you may wish to use it again in future semesters. The extra blank form will come in handy then.

Step 2: Complete a form of each of your courses.

Use the form to plan and write down the following information:

- On what days or dates do you plan to study for this course?
- For how long do you plan to study for this course during each study session?
- At what time of day (from x time to y time) do you plan to study for this course? (Time must not overlap with other courses or responsibilities.)
- In what types of study activities will you engage during the study sessions? Be specific. (For example, don't simply report that you will read the textbook; instead, note how many pages you will read during each session).

The forms you complete for this assignment will provide you with the information needed to complete the next assignment (see Assignment 2.3), which is related to the creation of a weekly study appointment sheet. Also the information you include in the strategy section of these forms will provide you with ideas for the study session tickets (task lists) that you will create in Assignment 2.4.

Assignment 2.2
Study Time Management Worksheet for a Single Course

Student Name:	Course:
Date:	Credit Hours:

Meeting Days and Times for the Course:

Details of the Study Plan:

WHEN will you study?

What Days?	*What Times?*		*How Long?*	
	Start	Finish		
Monday			hour(s)	minutes
Tuesday			hour(s)	minutes
Wednesday			hour(s)	minutes
Thursday			hour(s)	minutes
Friday			hour(s)	minutes
Saturday			hour(s)	minutes
Sunday			hour(s)	minutes
Weekly Total (Study Hours):			hour(s)	minutes

WHAT study strategies will you use? (List what you will do.)

1.

2.

3.

4.

5.

6.

7.

8.

9.

10.

Assignment 2.3

Weekly Appointment Sheet

Goal:

The purpose of this activity is to guide the student in the process of using information from the worksheets in Assignment 2.2 to a create single weekly appointment calendar sheet. The product will be a page that represents study appointments that the student can repeat each week during the semester.

Objective:

Based on information from Assignment 2.2, the student will create a weekly appointment sheet (calendar page) that designates, at a minimum, when he or she will study for each course and when he or she will attend each class.

Instructions:

Transfer the information from your **Study Time Management Worksheet for a Single Course** forms (provided with Assignment 2.2) onto the **Weekly Study Appointment Sheet** (provided on the following pages). The process for how to do this was described in Chapter 2. The basic idea is that you make an appointment with yourself to study for each course.

Follow these steps to fill in your **Weekly Study Appointment Sheet**:

Step 1: Draw and label boxes as necessary to indicate when you will be in class for the various courses that you are taking this semester. You can't change the time of the classes, and by virtue of enrolling you have made a commitment to attend at the times specified, so class time is a fixed commitment.

Step 2: Draw and label boxes to represent other commitments that you cannot change (such as your work schedule). Wait until after you complete Step 3 to indicate when you will handle commitments that are flexible with regard to time.

Step 3: Realize that this is a very important step. Draw and label boxes on the weekly schedule that indicate when you plan to study for each class. Do not simply indicate a generic study time; instead, specify exactly when you will study for each of your different classes.

Step 4: Make enough photocopies of the completed weekly schedule for you to have one for each week of the semester.

Step 5: Notice that the remaining blank spaces on your completed weekly appointment sheet (those not earmarked for studying or class meetings) represent your free time. Week by week you can use the free time slots to pencil in appointments or commitments that are flexible without letting those other commitments interfere with your study appointments.

NOTE: The study appointments that you created in Step 3 are appointments like any other, except that they are appointments that you have made with yourself. If you have to break a study appointment with yourself, remember to reschedule it for another time during that week so that you do not get behind in your studies.

Weekly Study Appointment Sheet

DATE →							
TIME ↓	Monday	Tuesday	Wednesday	Thursday	Friday	Saturday	Sunday
8 a.m.							
9 a.m.							
10 a.m.							
11 a.m.							
12 p.m.							
1 p.m.							
2 p.m.							
3 p.m.							
4 p.m.							
5 p.m.							
6 p.m.							
7 p.m.							

Weekly Study Appointment Sheet

DATE →							
TIME ↓	**Monday**	**Tuesday**	**Wednesday**	**Thursday**	**Friday**	**Saturday**	**Sunday**
8 a.m.							
9 a.m.							
10 a.m.							
11 a.m.							
12 p.m.							
1 p.m.							
2 p.m.							
3 p.m.							
4 p.m.							
5 p.m.							
6 p.m.							
7 p.m.							

Assignment 2.4

Study Session Tickets

Goal:

The purpose of this activity is to guide the student in the process of creating individual tickets for each study session he or she plans to have throughout the semester.

Objective:

Based on the description given in Chapter 2, the student will create a collection of study session tickets that can be used during the study sessions that he or she has planned.

Instructions:

Create as many tickets as necessary to use when you study for each class. This process was described earlier in Chapter 2.

Complete the following steps for each course separately:

Step 1: Look at your calendar to see when the next exam or assignment is due. Count how many study appointments you have made for yourself between now and the exam or other due date. You will need to make one ticket for each study session appointment.

Step 2: Decide what activities you will actually do during each study session. For example, for a history class you may do things like read the chapter, write outlines or draw tables to distinguish what information from the reading was most important, make flash cards to use when memorizing new vocabulary from this study session, and so on. For a math class you might do things such as read the chapter in the math textbook, work practice problems, create flash cards of theorems or formulas that you wish to memorize, and so on. If you are preparing to submit a research paper, then your task list for your first study session may simply read "select a topic," for the next session "find articles in the library," for the third session "read articles and make notes," and so on until you finish the paper.

Step 3: Write your tasks on the ticket. Before you write anything, you will need to make enough copies of the blank ticket template so that you will have one for each study session. For example, if you have made appointments with yourself to study for your psychology class on ten separate dates leading up to the date of the next psychology exam, then you would need to make ten copies of the template so that you can make a ticket for each study appointment.

If you develop a written study plan for each of your courses using the calendars and tickets as described in Chapter 2—and follow the plan—then you are likely to greatly improve your grades.

The next few pages in this book provide you with blank ticket forms. Several pages of tickets are provided in this book to get you started, but they will not be nearly enough to cover the entire semester. Therefore, you should make enough photocopies of these tickets so that you will be able to complete a separate ticket for each time you study for each course. It is important that you take a deliberate and active approach to studying and that you follow a plan that will result in getting the job done. These tools will help you.

Figure 2.5 Example of Ticket before and after Study Session

Example before Study Session

Study Session Ticket	
Name: *Jeefus Strickland*	
Course: *Sociology*	
Date: *M 9/17* **Time:** *2–4 pm*	
❑ 1.	*Check online for announcements*
❑ 2.	*Review & update notes from class*
❑ 3.	*Review notes made about Ch 1*
❑ 4.	*Review Ch 2 learning goals (pg. 64)*
❑ 5.	*Read Ch 2 (pp. 64–76)*
❑ 6.	*Make notes (find answers) about learning goals from reading*
Questions to ask in class:	

Example after Study Session

Study Session Ticket	
Name: *Jeefus Strickland*	
Course: *Sociology*	
Date: *M 9/17* **Time:** *2–4 pm*	
☑ 1.	*Check online for announcements*
☑ 2.	*Review & update notes from class*
☑ 3.	*Review notes made about Ch 1*
☑ 4.	*Review Ch 2 learning goals (pg. 64)*
☑ 5.	*Read Ch 2 (pp. 64–76)*
☑ 6.	*Make notes (find answers) about learning goals from reading*
Questions to ask in class:	
Ask professor to explain the difference between validity and reliability.	
***Note:** Had to quit early and didn't finish goals so I need to add extra 30 minutes and 6 more pages to next session to catch up.*	

Study Session Ticket

Name:

Course:

Date: Time:

❑ 1.

❑ 2.

❑ 3.

❑ 4.

❑ 5.

❑ 6.

❑ 7.

❑ 8.

❑ 9.

❑ 10.

Questions to ask in class:

Study Session Ticket

Name:

Course:

Date: Time:

❑ 1.

❑ 2.

❑ 3.

❑ 4.

❑ 5.

❑ 6.

❑ 7.

❑ 8.

❑ 9.

❑ 10.

Questions to ask in class:

Chapter 3 Roadmap

Listening and Taking Notes: Do You Hear What I Hear?

In this chapter you will learn techniques for effective listening and note taking. This chapter addresses these skills as a complete cycle—beginning with preparation for class, followed by listening and note-taking skills, and ending with strategies for review.

This chapter roadmap page presents the formal learning goals and a checklist that you should follow as you read and study the chapter.

Student Learning Goals for This Chapter

After completing this chapter you should be able to do the following:

1. Describe the nature of the cycle of learning, including the characteristics of each stage (before class, during class, after class).
2. Compare and contrast half listening, sound listening, and active listening.
3. Describe the characteristics of active listening.
4. Explain the ways in which effective listening involves behaviors from all three stages of the cycle of learning.
5. Describe the page layout used for the Cornell Method of Note Taking.
6. Define the components of the Cornell Method of Note Taking—including Record, Reduce, Recite, Reflect, and Review.
7. Explain when and how each of the components of the Cornell Method of Note Taking may be applied to a lecture class.
8. Demonstrate the ability to practice active listening and effective note taking in college.

Checklist for This Chapter

Target date/ deadline	Check when completed	Activity
________	❑	1. Complete Critical Thinking Activity 3.1.
________	❑	2. Convert the learning goals above to questions that you can answer as you read the chapter. Write your questions on the study guide pages near the end of this chapter.
________	❑	3. Read the chapter.
________	❑	4. Try to answer the reading comprehension questions as you come to them in the chapter. Check each answer by comparing it to the list of correct answers in the back of the book. If any answer was not correct, then review the passages preceding the question to see why you missed the question.
________	❑	5. Use the study guide pages near the end of this chapter to write down the answers to the questions you created in Step 2. Once completed, these answered questions will be your study guide.
________	❑	6. Write down any questions, insights, or comments that you have as you read so that you can bring them up in class (if applicable).
________	❑	7. Complete Review Questions 3.1.
________	❑	8. Complete Assignment 3.1 (Practice Note Taking)

CRITICAL THINKING ACTIVITY 3.1

Please answer the following true-false questions as a way to begin thinking about the topic of this chapter.

True or **False** 1. I am in class almost every day.

True or **False** 2. I participate in class.

True or **False** 3. I take notes in class.

True or **False** 4. I review my notes every day.

After you have answered, consider the analysis below.

Did you answer true to question number 1?

Being "in class" means that you are really present during the class period. This involves staying focused during class time, staying alert and awake, completing assigned readings in advance of class, and trying to understand and relate to the topic being discussed.

Did you answer true to question number 2?

Participating in class is an active process that includes asking questions about course content in class. Active participation is a very important component in effective listening because it helps you get more out of the class than you might otherwise. We will explore this further later in the chapter.

Question number 3 asks about taking notes during class.

Have you ever felt like you did not know what to write down when you took notes in class? Have you ever had difficulty understanding your notes when it was time to study for a test? Would you say that it is sometimes difficult for you to read your own handwriting when you try to study your notes? If your answer is "yes" for any of these questions, then this chapter is designed with you in mind.

Question number 4 asks about reviewing the notes you take in class.

Do you review your notes on a regular basis, or do you wait until the night before an exam to review them? Writing notes during class is a skill that you can work on, and it is important to develop effective strategies for actually using the notes that you take during class.

Listening and Taking Notes: Do You Hear What I Hear?

3

Do you understand the words that are comin' out of my mouth?

— Chris Tucker (as Detective Carter in the movie "Rush Hour")[1]

He listens well who takes notes.

— Dante Alighieri, "The Divine Comedy"[2]

3.1 Listening for Success

Effective listening involves behaviors from all three stages of the cycle of learning. Effective listening begins with preparation before class and ends with review after class.

As previously explained, at the college level approximately two-thirds of learning occurs outside of class and about one-third of learning occurs during class. Figure 3.1 illustrates the cycle of learning.

Figure 3.1 The Cycle of Learning

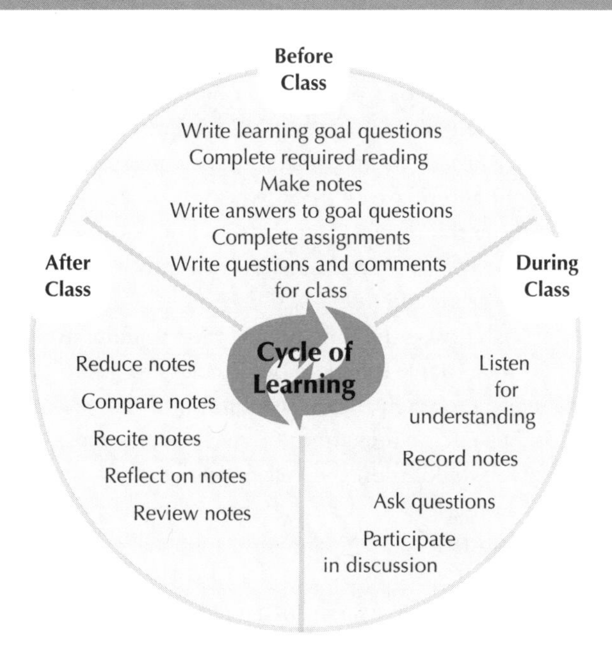

A. Preparing to Listen

Preparing to listen involves completing out-of-class assignments, removing distractions, and doing everything that you can to position yourself in the classroom for the most effective listening experience. This advance preparation is critical if you wish to listen effectively and gain maximum benefit from the lecture or class discussion.

1. Complete required reading and other assignments in advance

Effective listening starts long before the class begins. Completing the assigned reading prior to class is one way to prepare for effective listening. Most college courses require students to complete reading assignments and/or other learning activities before each class session. The syllabus for the course almost always contains a table or list identifying which readings are associated with each class session. Students are expected to complete the required reading or other learning activity (such as solving math problems) prior to the class session in which the reading is discussed. Students who complete the reading assignment before class are better able to understand and retain information presented in the lecture or discussion because the advanced reading gives them a foundation from which to approach the topic. In contrast, students who do not read in advance often feel "lost" during the lecture. The unprepared student may perceive the lecture as being "too fast" and may experience difficulty keeping up with the speaker.

2. Prepare questions in advance

As you complete the required reading or solve practice math problems, you are likely to discover that you have questions about the material. It is wise to write these questions down and take them to class with you. If your question is not automatically answered in the lecture, you can pose the question to the professor during or at the conclusion of the class. Writing your questions down when they occur to you will help you to remember them during class, and getting answers to all of your questions will improve your performance on exams.

3. Prepare your physical environment in advance

Arrive early so that you can get a good seat. It is often the case in college classes that students are allowed to sit anywhere they choose in the class. An important way to prepare to listen is to choose a seat that allows you to see and to hear clearly. Position yourself in such a way that you can more easily tune out any distractions. This usually means selecting a seat near the front and middle of the class, close to the speaker and to any audio visual presentations that the professor may offer.

You may have limited control over some aspects of the physical environment, such as the seating arrangements; however, you can control the part of the environment that you bring with you: your notebook, planner, textbook, pen, highlighter, cell phone, PDA, iPod, computer, and appropriate attire. *Remember: Bring to class all the supplies that you will need to listen, take notes, and participate in class discussion.* Make sure that your pens and highlighters are in good working order before class. Consider turning off, disabling, or leaving at home anything that might distract from your academic listening experience. Always bring your planner so that you are ready to immediately record information about exam dates, lab assignments, or other announcements that are made in class.

If you arrive early, you may wish to use the time before class to compare your notes from previous lessons with a classmate. It is a good idea to use this time before class to get to know some of your classmates because it sets the stage for a team approach to the listening and discussion that will take place during class. However, once class begins, all personal chatting (as well as text messaging, listening to music, playing computer games, surfing the web, talking on the cell phone, and eating snacks) should stop—and you should focus all of your attention on the lesson at hand. Some students pop a sugar-free lifesaver or breath mint into their mouths when class starts as a silent signal to themselves that it is time to stop chatting and start listening.

Many colleges have an emergency alert system for faculty, staff, and students that allows the college to send messages via cell phones, text messaging, and email to notify the campus community about severe weather, campus closing, or other emergencies. Cell phones are usually permitted in class because they are used by the college for emergency notifications. However, before class starts, you should set your cell phone to silent or vibrate mode so that it does not distract you or others during the lecture or discussion. If there is a campus emergency, then everyone's phone (including the professor's phone) will ring at the same time. You must respond to emergencies, but you should delay responding to all other communications until after class is over if you wish to be an effective listener.

Reading Comprehension Question 3.1 (Knowledge)

Preparing to listen in a class would include all EXCEPT which of the following activities?

a. Completing the required reading and other assignments before class.
b. Preparing questions in advance.
c. Preparing your physical environment in advance.
d. Having electronic devices, such as an iPad, prepared ahead for writing emails and notes to classmates.

B. Active Listening During Class

Deb Peterson has suggested that there are three levels of listening: half listening, sound listening, and active listening.[3] If you doodle, chat with others, tune out part of the time, or allow yourself to be distracted during the lecture, then you are only half listening. If you find yourself hearing the words but failing to comprehend the message or the meaning, then you are only listening to the sounds. Active listening is characterized by an engaged disposition. The active listener ignores distractions, makes eye contact with the speaker, keeps an open mind, focuses on the message rather than the speaker, seeks to understand the message, asks questions when appropriate, and remains engaged while taking notes.

Numerous writers have identified habits that detract from effective listening.[4] Some of these poor listening habits include defining the topic as boring, tolerating internal and external distractions, half listening, sound listening, trying to write down everything verbatim, focusing on points of disagreement, criticizing the speaker, listening only for facts rather than meaning, failing to ask questions, failing to participate in discussion, and failing to take notes. If you are aware of these problem behaviors, you can avoid them and instead practice active listening.

1. Avoid defining the topic as dull

Some professors and some topics may seem lack-luster, especially when compared to current advancements in the entertainment industry. However, whether or not the subject or speaker is dull isn't relevant to the successful student. The successful student takes personal responsibility to learn regardless of the quality or appeal of the presentation.

2. Avoid distractions

Distractions abound in the classroom. Internal distractions are personal issues that you may have been dwelling on during the day, such as financial problems, dating or marriage relationship problems, and grade anxiety. Internal distractions are sometimes difficult to dismiss. Try to compartmentalize your thinking. When you enter a class, try to mentally put yourself in a frame of mind that will allow you to focus on learning. Tell yourself, "Right now, I am now going to clear my mind and focus on the lesson until this class is over—and then I will deal with these problems."

External distractions are things in the physical environment that draw your attention away from the lesson, such as the temperature of the room, the noise in the room, the fact that someone you find extremely attractive just sat down next to you, and the professor's goofy hair or tie. You may not be able to do much about the professor's hair unless you are a cosmetologist, but you can often take simple steps to reduce other distractions. Select a seat that places your love interest out of your immediate view (at least for the duration of the class). If the class is always cold, bring a sweater. If people are making unnecessary noise chatting, you could respond by politely asking them to keep it down, moving away from them and closer to the professor, or asking the professor to address the problem.

3. Don't let points of disagreement stop you from listening

It is almost certain that you will hear things in college lectures with which you disagree—sometimes strongly. That is okay. Being a college student does not mean that you have to agree with everything that the professor says. Professors often disagree with one another. Professors sometimes present many alternative views in a lesson or course, even if they do not personally embrace some of those views. Learning about a variety of views and theories and learning to think about them critically are part of what a college-level education is all about. F. Scott Fitzgerald said, "The test of first rate intelligence is the ability to hold two opposing ideas at the same time and still retain the ability to function."[5] Don't allow your reaction to one point in the lecture distract you from actively listening to the rest of the lecture and learning what you need to know. The Elmhurst College Learning Center recommends, "Hear the speaker out ... Don't jump to conclusions ... Don't stop listening because of an emotional response to a word or topic," and "Don't give up because the subject is difficult."

4. Engage the professor and others in the class

An important part of active listening is asking and answering questions. Since the goal of active listening is to ensure that you understand the message, it is often necessary to ask questions for clarification. There may be portions of the class period when it would be inappropriate to interrupt the speaker with a question, but effective teaching and learning cannot take place unless some portion of the class is set aside for questions and discussion. In most cases, the professor's lecture is organized into a number of sections (covering several different points). Most professors are prepared to entertain questions following each of these sections during their lecture. Unfortunately, students often remain silent at these times. Many students also appear reluctant to answer questions that are posed to the class by the professor. Researchers have documented this nationwide trend of timidity among students when it comes to discussion in class and have labeled the phenomenon "the silent college classroom."[6] Recent research has found that typically only about 25 percent of students participate in classroom discussion while the rest of the students remain silent.[7] One way that you, as an individual, can overcome this handicap is to write questions in your notes. If any questions come to your mind during the lecture, or if anything about the lecture is unclear to you, write it down in your notes. Then you will be ready to introduce your question when the class discussion starts. You should also jot down any questions you think of during your preparatory reading before class. Then if they are not answered by the lecture, you can introduce them during the class discussion.

Want to learn more?

Take the brief personal assessment surveys at the following URL (Elmhurst College):
Barriers to Effective Listening Survey
http://bvtlab.com/66F6J

Read more about listening techniques at the following URLs:
How to Listen and Retain: Active Listening Tips, by Grace Fleming
http://bvtlab.com/8h8qj
Listening, L.I.S.T.E.N. (California Polytechnic State University)
http://bvtlab.com/a78g6

Taking notes is also part of active listening. Taking notes is one way to improve your listening and retain more information from class. It could be said that note taking is an extension of listening.

Reading Comprehension Question 3.2 (Literal Comprehension)

How is active listening different from half listening?

a. Active listeners keep an open mind, focus on the message, and keep an engaged disposition.
b. Active listeners sometimes write notes to their classmates during class.
c. Half listening requires engagement and attention.
d. Active listening results in a better understanding of what is being said during the lecture.
e. a and d

3.2 Taking Notes for Success

Has anyone ever formally taught you how to take notes in class? One professor has posed that question to classes of freshmen students on the first day of class for more than ten years—always with the same results. Very few, and often none, of the freshmen in his classes recalled ever being taught how to take notes. Perhaps this reflects a general, widely held misconception that note taking is so simple that it requires no instruction. The truth is that effective note taking is a skill that must be learned and can be improved upon. This section of the chapter will suggest some methods and principles of effective note taking that will help you improve this skill.

This chapter will describe the Cornell Method and offer some guidelines for effective note taking. There are many "formulas" for how to take notes that have been proposed in the academic literature. Ultimately the best method, however, is the method that works best for you as an individual and best fits your own learning style.

A. The Cornell Method of Note Taking

One tried and true method for taking notes is known as the Cornell Method.[8] It was developed decades ago by professor Walter Pauk, who served as director of the Reading-Study Center at Cornell University. The Cornell Method involves dividing the note page into three sections. One of the sections is used for taking notes in class, and the other sections are used to record questions and update the notes during the review and study process.

Figure 3.2 Diagram of the Cornell Method of Note Taking

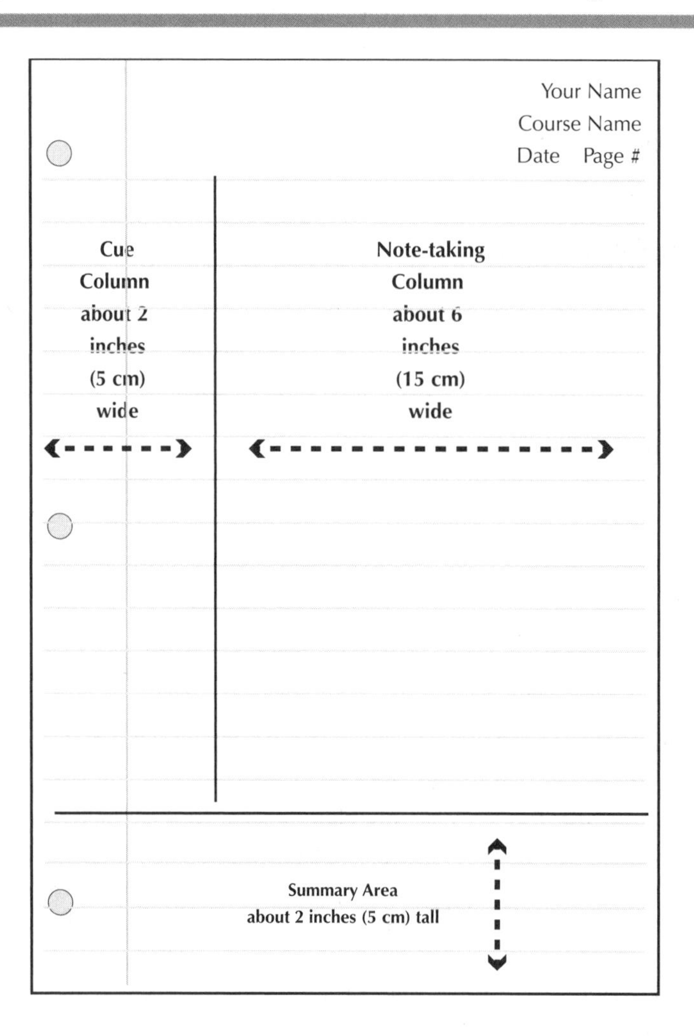

As is illustrated in Figure 3.2, when using the Cornell method you must draw one vertical line and one horizontal line on your note page so that it is divided into three sections: a cue section, a note-taking section, and a summary section. The horizontal line should be drawn about two inches (5 cm) above the bottom of the page. The space below the horizontal line is the **summary area**. The vertical line should divide the space above the summary section into two columns. The vertical line should be drawn about two inches (5 cm) from the left side of the page. It should extend from the top of the page to the horizontal line. The space to the left of the vertical line is called the **cue column**, and the space to the right of the vertical line is called the **note-taking column**. Since a standard piece of notebook paper is 8.5 inches wide, you should have a cue column that is approximately two inches (5 cm) wide and a note-taking column that is approximately six inches (15 cm) wide. Always label each page with your name, the title of the course, the date, and the page number. This **identification label** will be especially helpful if you use loose-leaf pages because it will make it easier to keep the pages organized and in order. Pauk described note taking as a five-step process. The 5 R's of note taking include (1) Record, (2) Reduce, (3) Recite, (4) Reflect, and (5) Review.

Figure 3.3 Example of a Note Page During Class

Jane Doe
Sociology 1101
January 13, 2014 Page 1 of _____

Sociology
Sociology is the scientific study of society and social interaction.

1. What Sociology is NOT
A. Casual observation

Casual observation is a good place to start but we often see only the surface reality.

B. Common Sense

Common sense is vague, contradictory and unreliable.

Sociology is —specific
-based on (empirical ?) research

Reading Comprehension Question 3.3 (Inferential Comprehension)

Why is the Cornell Method of Note Taking a good method?

a. It helps the student write down the instructor's words, verbatim.
b. It has been used for many years.
c. It allows the student to accomplish homework while taking notes during class.
d. It provides a way for the student to take notes, review the notes, and study after class.

Step 1: Record (during class)

Use the note-taking column to record your notes during class. Leave the cue column and the summary area blank until after class. This is illustrated in Figure 3.3. Following are a few tips that will help you record your notes effectively during class:

- Arrive early. If you are late, you may miss important information.
- Sit in the front and middle of the class so that you can hear better, see better, and block out distractions more easily.
- Avoid carrying on conversations, sending or reading text messages, surfing the web, daydreaming, sleeping, or letting anything distract you during class when you should be listening and taking notes.
- Listen carefully with understanding as your goal. If you obsessively copy down every word but do not understand what you are writing, then your notes will not serve you well as a study tool. Do not try to write down everything that the professor says but instead identify the important concepts that you will need to help you study later. Your goal when taking notes should be to create an outline or paraphrase of what the professor has said.
- Look for cues as to what points the professor thinks are most important. These include structural cues (such as transition words), non-verbal cues (body language), visual cues (such as when the professor provides a handout or writes on the board), and phonological cues (such as when the professor changes volume or repeats information).
- Write legibly. Some students prefer to write in cursive because it is faster while others prefer to print in block letters because it is easier to read later. Experiment and see what works better for you, but make sure that you will be able to read and understand what you have written when you study.
- Skip one line between ideas and several lines between topics so that you will have some space to add a note or two later if needed.
- Use symbols and abbreviations to save time, but be sure that you write in such a way that you can read and understand it with ease later.
- Ask questions. Most professors allow time for questions, and many encourage students to ask questions. Take advantage of this opportunity to ask for clarification of difficult points or simply to fill in information you missed. The chances are high that other students in the class also need to hear the answer. Therefore, asking your questions will help the professor teach better, and it will help everyone learn better. In answer to your questions, the professor may discuss the material in different words or add illustrations that will simplify the material. Take notes on his or her answers.
- Make sure to get the information that you need to learn the material and to prepare for exams. If you missed something that the professor said, ask him or her to repeat it or go to the professor after class and ask for clarification. If you are in a rush after class, you can ask the professor at the beginning of the next class or try to find the answer from a friend or from the textbook. If that does not work, make an appointment and visit the professor during office hours.

A University of Washington website provides the following advice for students who may have trouble taking notes:

> If you have trouble taking notes, find someone in the class who takes good notes and ask if they would be willing to give you a copy of them. Continue to take your own notes because listening to the lecture and writing notes at the same time helps you remember the information better. Then check your notes against the other set of notes after class. Look at the information your classmate is recording, and use this example to improve your note-taking skills. You may also want to consider tape recording lectures and then listening to the tapes while reviewing both sets of notes. Be sure to obtain the lecturer's permission before taping a lecture.

Figure 3.4 Example of a Note Page after Class

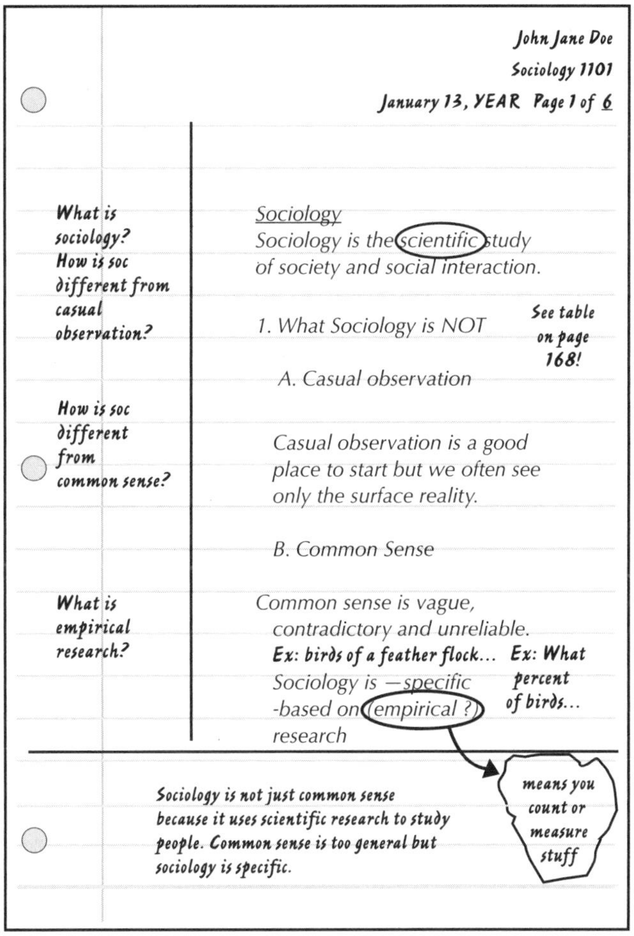

John Jane Doe
Sociology 1101
January 13, YEAR Page 1 of 6

Cue column	Notes
What is sociology? How is soc different from casual observation?	Sociology Sociology is the scientific study of society and social interaction. 1. What Sociology is NOT — See table on page 168! A. Casual observation
How is soc different from common sense?	Casual observation is a good place to start but we often see only the surface reality. B. Common Sense
What is empirical research?	Common sense is vague, contradictory and unreliable. Ex: birds of a feather flock... Ex: What percent of birds... Sociology is —specific -based on (empirical ?) research

Sociology is not just common sense because it uses scientific research to study people. Common sense is too general but sociology is specific.

means you count or measure stuff

Step 2: Reduce (immediately after class)

As soon as possible after class, use the cue column to write down questions based on your notes. Pauk explains that writing questions will help you to "clarify meanings, reveal relationships, establish continuity, and strengthen memory."[9] Also at this time, you should tidy up your notes by adding any information that you did not have time to write down in class. You may need to add definitions to words that you don't know, spell out the meaning of unusual abbreviations, or clarify any other ambiguous information. In addition, you should write a short summary of the notes in the summary area at the bottom of the page. The Reduce process is illustrated in Figure 3.4.

You need to perform this step as soon as possible after class. Try to do it immediately after class while it is fresh in your mind because if you wait until after dinner that night you are likely to have forgotten some of it already. The remaining three steps (Recite, Reflect, and Review) should be done at a later time—the time you have scheduled to study for this class.

It is also a good idea to compare your notes to those of a classmate on a regular basis. It may be that your classmate included something in his or her notes that you inadvertently overlooked. When you compare notes, you can add that information to your own notes.

Step 3: Recite (during a routine study session prior to the next class)

Recite means to read aloud. When you sit down to study your notes, you can use the questions that you have written in the cue column as a way to begin learning the material. Cover the note-taking column with a piece of paper so that you cannot see it. Then as you read down the cue column, say the answers to the questions aloud. Lift the cover to confirm the accuracy of your answers.

Step 4: Reflect (during a routine study session)

Reflect means to think. It is important that you take time during your study session to think about the information that you have learned. In order to master a college-level course, the student must do more than simply memorize definitions or facts. The student must strive to understand the concepts. Pauk suggested that students ask themselves questions such as the following: "What is the significance of these facts? What principle are they based on? How can I apply them? How do they fit in with what I already know?"[12]

Step 5: Review (during every routine study session)

Finally, it is very important that you schedule time every night or week to review all your previous notes. Each time you review, start at the beginning (i.e., the first page of notes that you wrote for the class or unit) and review the notes for each day until the current date. This process does not take as much time as you might assume because the more times you read the same material, the faster you can read it. This day-to-day review process will enable you to develop greater understanding of the important concepts and actually learn rather than simply memorizing. Then the knowledge will be recorded not just in your short-term memory but in your long-term memory as well.

Reading Comprehension Question 3.4 (Analysis)

Which of the following is true of note taking in college?

a. Students who take notes every class will have a record of attending all their classes.
b. Good notes provide material for in-depth studying of the course content.
c. Good notes are not as important as reading the textbook.
d. All of the above

Want to learn more?

Try these resources.

You can view a description and see examples of the Cornell Note-taking System at the following URLs:
http://bvtlab.com/DYc6S
http://bvtlab.com/47Bq7
http://bvtlab.com/P8aPq

You can download Microsoft Word templates to create Cornell note-taking pages at the following URL:
http://bvtlab.com/N6e72

You can create Cornell note-taking pages in PDF format at the following URLs:
http://bvtlab.com/86777
Graph paper version:
http://bvtlab.com/88287

Summary

In this chapter you learned about two valuable skills in the cycle of learning: active listening and note taking. Students who practice half listening or sound listening will not be as well equipped to succeed in college as students who practice active listening. Effective listening actually begins before class with preparation. During class, the active listener ignores distractions, makes eye contact with the speaker, keeps an open mind, focuses on the message rather than the speaker, seeks to understand the message, asks questions when appropriate, and remains engaged while taking notes. Note-taking skills can be learned, practiced, and improved upon. The Cornell Method of Note Taking system is recommended. The Cornell Method of Note Taking involves a five-step process for note taking: Record, Reduce, Recite, Reflect, and Review. The cycle of learning is completed as the student reviews and studies his or her notes. Reviewing and studying your notes should be part of your routine study plan for each course that you take. The particulars of how to develop a study plan were discussed in Chapter 2.

The assignment for this chapter will be to use the blank note-taking page provided to take notes for one of your classes or at a public event with a speaker.

Review Questions 3.1

Instructions: Following are five true-false statements taken from the information in this chapter. First, try to answer them without looking back at the chapter. Then review the chapter to see how well you did.

Question & Answer	Rationale
Circle true or false for each of the following statements.	**Write an explanation stating why each statement is true or false.**
1. Effective listening starts as soon as you enter the classroom. **True or False**	Your Rationale:
2. The goal of active listening is to ensure that you will be able to write down everything that the professor says. **True or False**	Your Rationale:
3. Part of the Cornell Method of Note Taking is reading your notes aloud. **True or False**	Your Rationale:
4. Reviewing your class notes once before an exam is enough to encode them in your long-term memory. **True or False**	Your Rationale:
5. This chapter explains that the best method for note taking is the Cornell Method of Note Taking. **True or False**	Your Rationale:

Name: ___________________________

Chapter Three **Study Guide**

Chapter 3, Goal 1: The student will be able to describe the nature of the cycle of learning, including the characteristics of each stage (before class, during class, after class).

Questions	Answers & Notes

Name: ______________________________

Chapter Three

Study Guide

Chapter 3, Goal 2: The student will be able to compare and contrast half listening, sound listening, and active listening.

Questions	Answers & Notes

Name: ________________________________

Chapter Three

Study Guide

Chapter 3, Goal 3: The student will be able to describe the characteristics of active listening.

Questions	Answers & Notes

Name: ______________________

Chapter Three

Study Guide

Chapter 3, Goal 4: The student will be able to explain the ways in which effective listening involves behaviors from all three stages of the cycle of learning.

Questions	Answers & Notes

Name: ____________________

Chapter Three

Study Guide

Chapter 3, Goal 5: The student will be able to describe the page layout used for the Cornell Method of Note Taking.

Questions	Answers & Notes

Name: ________________________________

Chapter Three

Study Guide

Chapter 3, Goal 6: The student will be able to define the components of the Cornell Method of Note Taking—Record, Reduce, Recite, Reflect, and Review.

Questions	Answers & Notes

Name: ____________________

Chapter Three **Study Guide**

Chapter 3, Goal 7: The student will be able to explain when and how each of the components of the Cornell Method of Note Taking may be applied to a lecture class.

Questions	Answers & Notes

Name: ____________________

Chapter Three

Study Guide

Chapter 3, Goal 8: The student will be able to demonstrate the ability to practice active listening and effective note taking in a college course.

Questions	Answers & Notes

Name: ________________________________

Preparing for Class:
Use This Page to Record Questions or Insights to Discuss in Class.

Assignment 3.1

Practice Taking Notes

Goal:

The purpose of this activity is for the student to master using the Cornell Method of Note Taking.

Objective:

The student will demonstrate understanding of the Cornell Method of Note Taking technique by using the technique to take notes for a class lecture, a workshop, or a public meeting.

Instructions:

Chapter 3 of this textbook explains a note-taking technique called the Cornell Method. Use information from Chapter 3 to practice taking notes.

Follow these steps:

Step 1: Review the Cornell Method of Note Taking in Chapter 3.

Step 2: Attend a class lecture, a workshop, or another meeting where a speaker is making a presentation, and use the Cornell Method of Note Taking to take notes at the meeting. Use the following page for this purpose.

Step 3: After the meeting, review your notes and compare them with the content in Chapter 3 to see if you understand how to take notes according to the Cornell Method of Note Taking.

Name: ______________________ ______________________ ______________ ____/____

Event Title | Date | Page

Chapter 4 Roadmap

Reading: What They Never Taught You in Kindergarten!

In this chapter you will learn how to improve one of the most important academic skills that you will use in college and in life—reading. Topics include how to effectively read textbooks and how to respond to new vocabulary. You will learn strategies for reading that have been proven by research to be most effective, such as the SOAR and SQ3R methods. You will be asked to practice these methods in the assignments associated with this chapter.

This chapter roadmap page presents the formal learning goals for this chapter and a checklist that you should follow as you read and study the chapter.

Student Learning Goals for This Chapter

After completing this chapter the student should be able to do the following:

1. Explain why reading textbooks in college is so important.
2. Demonstrate how to use a textbook effectively.
3. Describe strategies that can improve reading comprehension.
4. Demonstrate the practice of SOAR: (S) selecting important information from less important information when reading, (O) organizing the information in new ways, (A) associating or creating meaningful connections between ideas, and (R) regulating through practice and self-evaluation.
5. Apply the SQ3R method to a reading a passage.
6. Use concept mapping as a way to move beyond definitions to associations when learning new vocabulary.

Checklist for This Chapter

Target date/ deadline	Check when completed	Activity
________	❑	1. Complete Critical Thinking Activity 4.1.
________	❑	2. Convert the learning goals above to questions that you can answer as you read the chapter. Write your questions on the study guide pages near the end of this chapter.
________	❑	3. Read the chapter.
________	❑	4. Try to answer the reading comprehension questions as you come to them in the chapter. Check each answer by comparing it to the list of correct answers in the back of the book. If any answer was not correct, then review the passages preceding the question to see why you missed the question.
________	❑	5. Use the study guide pages near the end of this chapter to write down answers to the questions you created in Step 2. Once completed, these pages will be your study guide.
________	❑	6. Write down any questions, insights, or comments that you have as you read so that you can bring them up in class (if applicable).
________	❑	7. Complete Review Questions 4.1.
________	❑	8. Complete Assignment 4.1 (Identify New Vocabulary).

CRITICAL THINKING ACTIVITY 4.1

Following is a problem-solving question similar to those that students often face. Your responses to such problems could mean the difference between success and failure as a student—between graduating with a college degree and not graduating at all.

Suppose you can't afford to buy a textbook in time for the first day of classes. Going without a textbook is not an option. Use critical thinking and problem-solving skills to make a list of solutions (permanent or temporary) that will allow you to complete the assigned reading on schedule.

Write your list in the space provided on this page. Be prepared to share your ideas in class (if applicable).

Reading:

What They Never Taught You in Kindergarten!

No matter how busy you may think you are, you must find time for reading, or surrender yourself to self-chosen ignorance.

— *Confucius*[1]

Wear the old coat and buy the new book.

— *Austin Phelps*[1]

Which is more difficult to read, fiction or non-fiction?

While it is noteworthy that fiction and non-fiction are usually written in different styles, with different features, and in a different structure, the answer to this question may be partly dependent on the purpose behind your reading. If you encounter a difficult book when reading for pleasure, you may simply discontinue reading and switch to something easier. You will not have that option when it comes to the required reading assignments you have in college. While some of your assigned reading in college will include works of fiction, a substantial portion of the required reading will be a special type of book: the textbook. Even when reading fiction works in college, you will be required to think more deeply about those fictional books than you might if you were reading them for pleasure. In many cases the required reading in college will constitute both a challenge and a pleasure.

One of the most important activities that will occupy your time in college is reading. Reading is, in effect, the key to success in college.

In this chapter you will learn why reading textbooks is so important in college and how to use a textbook effectively. We will explore some reading and studying strategies, such as the research-proven SOAR method and the widely accepted SQ3R method. These principles will help you to read more effectively.

4.1 What Is Reading?

One definition of reading is: "Reading is not a simple, passive process of linear reading of words and internalizing their meaning one at a time. Reading is a complex interaction between the text and the reader shaped by the readers' prior knowledge and attitude, a process of language acquisition, communication and sharing information and ideas."[2]

Much can be written about reading in general, but our primary focus is to briefly identify principles and techniques that college students can apply to the reading of their textbooks.

TRY THIS!

In the left column below are a series of quotes about reading with the author identified. Use the space provided in the right column to write what message you think the author wanted to convey. Consider the author in your analysis.

Quote	Intended Message
"The more you read, the more things you will know. The more that you learn, the more places you'll go." – Dr. Seuss	
"Some people will lie, cheat, steal and back-stab to get ahead ... and to think, all they have to do is READ." – *Fortune*	
"Once you learn to read, you will be forever free." – Frederick Douglass	
"Not all readers are leaders, but all leaders are readers." – Harry S. Truman	
"The man who does not read good books has no advantage over the man who can't read." – Mark Twain	
"You don't have to burn books to destroy a culture. Just get people to stop reading them." – Ray Bradbury	
"Think before you speak. Read before you think." – Fran Lebowitz	
"Reading is to the mind what exercise is to the body." – Richard Steele	
"My alma mater was books, a good library … I could spend the rest of my life reading, just satisfying my curiosity." – Malcolm X	

Source: Quotes from The Literacy Company.

4.2 Why Textbooks?

Many introductory level textbooks are quite impressive in terms of the volume of information contained therein. Textbooks don't just present the core concepts of the discipline; they are also loaded with vignettes, boxed essays related to—but separate from—the body of the text, pictures, charts, tables, maps, and so on. These are all desirable components; taken together, however, they sometimes result in a book measuring over two inches thick and costing more than $200. It is easy to understand how a first-year college student taking five classes could be overwhelmed by the massive content (and cost)!

Nevertheless, making good use of your textbooks is without a doubt one of the most important skills you must learn. The textbook is absolutely essential for the vast majority of college courses. Failing to acquire and read a textbook is one of the biggest mistakes that a student can make in a course. If you are enrolled in a course for which you think the textbook is optional, ask the professor if he or she thinks that you will be able to perform well in the course without the textbook. If the professor agrees, then it will be fine. Otherwise, assume that the textbook is critical and not optional.

As the Austin Phelps' quote that began this chapter suggested, obtaining a textbook must be a budget priority for any student who wishes to be successful in college. Critical Thinking Activity 4.1 asked you to think of ways to complete the required reading assignment for a college course if you could not afford a textbook. Can you think of additional ways to obtain a textbook if you cannot afford to buy one? This is a problem that you might need to solve in order to be successful in college.

Reading Comprehension Question 4.1 (Knowledge)

Why are textbooks important in college?

a. Because introductory textbooks have all the information you need to pass that course
b. Because these books replace the professor's lecture materials for most classes
c. Because in most college courses, textbooks provide essential information for understanding and learning the course material
d. None of the above

In the next section of this chapter, we will explore how to read a college textbook effectively. Your attitude about reading will make a big difference in your likelihood of success. Table 4.1 presents statements associated with good and bad attitudes about reading. How many of the bad ideas do you agree with? How many of the good ideas do you agree with? If you want to be successful in college, you will need to abandon the bad ideas and adopt good ideas and behaviors regarding reading.

Table 4.1 Bad and Good Dispositions Toward Reading a Textbook

Bad Ideas	Good Ideas
I don't plan to buy (or otherwise acquire) a textbook.	I will make owning the textbook a top budget priority.
I will not buy a textbook on the first day of class, but I might buy one at some time later in the semester.	If I can't afford the book, then I will look for another way to acquire one so that I can complete the reading and adequately prepare for class.
I don't plan to read the textbook.	I will prepare to read by planning specific times in my schedule for that purpose.
Instead of reading, I will just skim the textbook to look for items that I think will be on the exam.	I will adopt a reading strategy such as SOAR or SQ3R to insure that my reading is effective.
I will wait until after the professor lectures on a chapter before I read the chapter so that I can use the lecture for clues about what parts of the book will be on the exam.	I will read the assignment before the class when it is the topic of lecture or discussion so that I will be prepared for each class and will not fall behind.
I expect the professor to go through the book during the class, before an exam, and to tell the students which pages are important. I will wait until then to read.	When we do discuss a chapter in class, I will ask questions about anything that I did not understand from my reading.
	I will take adult responsibility for my learning, and I will not expect the professor to spoon feed the information to me as if I were an elementary school child.

4.3 How to Read a Textbook

The first step for success in reading is to actually read the textbook. Too many students try to get through a course without actually reading. They may not buy a book and therefore not read at all, or they may acquire a book but never open it. Activities such as skimming, highlighting sentences when the professor reads them in class, or staring blankly at the page while in study hall do not constitute effective reading.

D'Agostino, a former mathematics and physics professor and textbook writer/editor, addressed the question of why students do not read textbooks in his blog.

> In the frenzy of deadline after deadline (assignments due, quizzes, tests, labs, lab reports, etc.), it's all they can do to put out the next fire. As a result, they are very inefficient; they can't take the time to do a good job of learning the material, which would involve reading the textbook, working through the examples, and doing many practice exercises. Instead, they devote far more time to completing the assignments than would be necessary if they had done many practice exercises, because they attempt the assignments before they really understand the material. But they don't see an alternative, because the assignments are worth marks, and so they are (unfortunately) a higher priority than actually learning the material. By the end of the course, they understand very little, even if they have managed to score a decent grade.[5]

Does D'Agostino's explanation fit your situation? Do you have trouble reading effectively? If so, can you identify any barriers that prevent you from reading success? In order to become a better reader, you should devote time to reading, treat reading as a top priority, seek a reading environment without distractions, and employ proven strategies such as the SOAR and SQ3R methods.

A. Expect to devote time to reading

Effective reading and studying take time. The number of hours that students spend studying has gradually decreased since the 1960s, from twenty-four hours per week in 1961 to fourteen hours per week in recent years.[3] We could hypothesize that students need less time to study today due to technological advances (after all, a calculator is faster than a slide rule); however, if so, then we would expect them to learn more and earn higher grades. They don't. Researchers have observed that, unaided, students make the same types of study errors using electronic media as they do using other media.[4] Bottom line: if you want to be successful in college, you are going to have to devote a lot of time to reading and studying.

B. Don't try to multitask

Any adult can understand why texting while driving is a serious mistake. The dangers of texting on your phone or another electronic device while reading your textbook may not be immediately apparent to some students, but it is also a big mistake. If you want to learn and be successful in college, then you are going to have to be so committed to studying that you are willing to turn off your phone, TV, music, or any other distraction while you study.

C. Read in an environment that supports studying

Are you planning to read and study in the dorms? ROFLMAO! No way. There are too many distractions and interruptions. Go to a place that will enable you to concentrate on your reading and studying. The library is usually a great place to study. Tutoring labs are also good. But it does not have to be a place labeled "study hall," as long as it is a place free from distractions, where you can read, think, take notes, and concentrate.

The Virginia Tech website has a *Study Environment Analysis* tool that lets you type in three locations and then evaluate them as reading locations by answering 12 simple questions. Try it yourself by browsing to the following URL: **http://bvtlab.com/GPe8Z**

D. Employ proven strategies for reading

There are many good strategies that you could adopt to improve your reading. In this book we will review two of them: the SOAR method and the SQ3R method. These methods are very useful when reading the typical textbook.

1. SOAR

Would you like to score twenty-nine to sixty-three points higher on your next exam? Through research, Kenneth Kiewra discovered four techniques that, when practiced by students while studying, significantly improve learning. They are known by the acronym SOAR which stands for Selecting, Organizing, Associating, and Regulating. **Selecting** refers to distinguishing what information is important.[5] **Organizing** involves converting information from its initial form to comparative charts and illustrations.[6] **Associating** involves creating meaningful connections between ideas.[7] **Regulating** includes learning through practice and self-evaluation.[8] Kiewra found that "undergraduates in the study scored 29 to 63 percentage points higher on tests when they used study techniques like recording complete notes, creating comparative charts, building associations, and crafting practice questions."[9]

Table 4.2		Description of the SOAR Model
S	Select	Distinguish important information from the information that is less important.
O	Organize	Convert the important information into another format such as a table, list, chart, timeline, etc. that reflects your understanding of the main points.
A	Associate	Recognize the connections between the different important facts, ideas, or concepts.
R	Regulate	Assess yourself at regular intervals to determine how much of the important material you have adequately learned. When you discover a gap in your knowledge or a deficiency in the quality of your understanding, engage in additional learning to correct the problem.

Sources: Jairam& Kiewra 2009; Jairam & Kiewra 2010; Kiewra 2002; Kiewra 2005; and University of Nebraska-Lincoln 2010, August 10

As Kiewra noted, "Learning occurs best when important information is selected from less important ideas, when selected information is organized graphically, when associations are built among ideas, and when understanding is regulated through self-testing."[10] The elements of SOAR can be incorporated into a popular method called SQ3R.[2]

2. SQ3R

Effectively reading a college textbook or journal article involves a lot more than simply moving your eyes across the page and decoding the words. This is illustrated by a summary of the SQ3R method.[11] SQ3R stands for Survey, Question, Read, Review, and Recite.[12] The principles of the SOAR method can be incorporated into the SQ3R strategy.

2a. Survey

Using this method, you should begin your reading assignment by **surveying** what you are expected to read to get a general overview of it. Observe how the document is organized or divided. Textbooks often include reading tools embedded into the chapter to help you read more effectively. Look to see what reading tools are included in the document, such as a list of learning goals for the chapter, a list of key terms, definitions set out in the margins, the important terms or phrases printed in bold, an outline, or a summary. Surveying the document before reading will help you to distinguish the most relevant information from any less relevant parts (this is referred to as **Selecting** in the SOAR model).

2b. Question

"Question" means to actively engage with the text by asking yourself questions before and while you read. Examples of questions you might ask include the following: What is this chapter about? What is the main idea? What facts support the main idea? What examples are given? What information in this chapter is relevant and important? What information will help me address the **learning goals** for the course, chapter, or lesson? Clearly stated goals for each chapter can help students with the very important study task of determining what facts or concepts presented in the reading or lecture are most important. If the goals are not already provided for you in the textbook, the syllabus, or in a handout from the professor, then ask the professor what his or her goals are for the chapter or lesson in question.

2c. Read

Once your survey of the document is complete, you are ready to begin **reading** sections of it. Especially in the case of reading a textbook, you should write notes about what you are reading. Do not write everything, but instead isolate the most important points and organize them in a way that makes sense to you. Yep, effective reading involves writing! The point of this note-taking is to shrink the important content of the chapter down to a few brief summary pages that will help you learn the information. You should try to convert the information from its initial form to comparative charts and illustrations—this is called **Organizing** in the SOAR model).

Note-taking will help you concentrate on your reading. Sometimes this reading will move along quickly, especially when you are covering familiar material. At other times you will need to slow down and concentrate to make sure that you understand what you are reading. Understanding is paramount. While it is true that some things—such as special vocabulary—should be memorized, the main objective of your reading should be to learn and understand the content.

2d. Review

At the college level, reading something one time usually isn't enough to master it. This is where the notes you take while reading come in handy. You should plan time to **review** them on a regular basis. Difficult material may need to be reviewed more often than less challenging material. When you review, try to make connections between the information in your notes, information in other reading assignments, information from lectures, and information from class discussions—(this is called **Association** in the SOAR model). This is a very important part of the process because it will help you to elevate your studying from the level of memorization to the level of critical thinking and understanding.

2e. Recite

Recite means to say the information out loud or to write it out on paper. In order to get the full benefit from your reading, you should set aside time each week to recite your notes. This is an activity that can be done with a partner who is learning the same material. Hearing another person's notes may help you to improve your understanding and memory of the information—even more so than if you used just your own notes. Use your notes to test yourself. (The act of learning through practice and self-evaluation is called **Regulating** in the SOAR model.)

Want to learn more?

Try these resources.

View the video called *Reading Improvement* (10:48 minutes, captioned) at the following URL:
http://bvtlab.com/879n6
This video is presented by the Academic Skills Center at Dartmouth College. The Dartmouth site has a number of additional videos and written (downloadable) resources that address student success.

Download the list of *Active Reading Strategies* from the McGraw Center for Teaching and Learning at Princeton University, at the following URL:
http://bvtlab.com/4cNb7

Reading Comprehension Question 4.2 (Literal Comprehension)

Why is it important that students use the SOAR method of reading and studying?

a. Students should use it because any method is better than no method.
b. Students should use it because it is the most recent method developed by reading experts.
c. Research has been proven that students score much higher on tests when they use the SOAR method.
d. It is not recommended that students use the SOAR method; they are urged to use the more popular SQ3R method, instead.

4.4 Road Signs for Reading

Effective reading is a stop-and-go process. Efficient readers vary their reading according to the material being read and their purpose for reading it. Some reading material is intended to be read faster, such as magazines or newspapers. Textbooks are generally read more slowly, but even within textbooks there are passages that can be read quickly. Following are some general tips to help you read more efficiently:

1. **Merge: Read phrases instead of individual words.** Normally when you read you will be able to read faster and comprehend better if you focus your eyes on groups of words that make up phrases instead of focusing on each word individually.

2. **Slow down for difficult passages.** Avoid reading the same phrase over and over without understanding it. Instead, if you are dealing with a difficult passage in a book, slow down, concentrate, and read the passage more carefully. In the long run, it may take less time to read a difficult passage slowly with understanding than it would to read it many times quickly without understanding.

3. **Stop to think about what you have read.** Periodically, as you read, you should stop and think about what you have read. What was the point of the passage? What part of it is most important? What did you learn by reading it? Was there any part of it that did not make sense to you? Was there any vocabulary that is new to you (that you need to look up)? Do you need to write notes about anything in the passage?

4. **Speed up for easier material.** You may read faster when dealing with not-so-difficult passages of the text. In other words, you should vary your reading rate and technique so that it matches the difficulty level and writing style of the passage.

Reading Comprehension Question 4.3 (Inferential Comprehension)

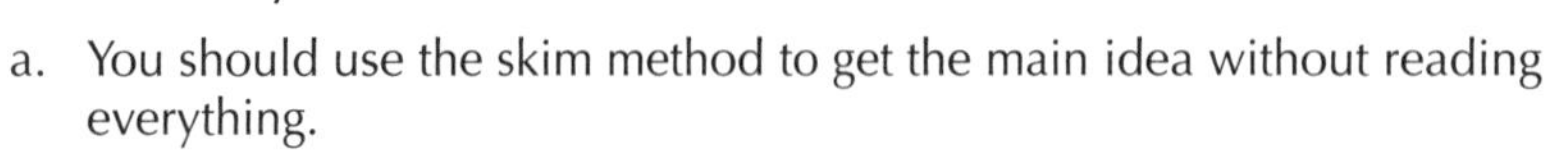

Based on the information in the above passage called "Road Signs for Reading," how should you read a textbook?

a. You should use the skim method to get the main idea without reading everything.

b. You should read the textbook slowly, line by line

c. You should read as fast as you can because college students have a large amount of required reading.

d. You should vary your reading rate and technique so that it matches the difficulty level and writing style of the passage.

4.5 Responding to New Vocabulary

No matter how much education you acquire, as long as you keep reading, you will continue to encounter new vocabulary. This is positive because it means that you are learning new things. How do you identify new vocabulary? Once you have identified new vocabulary, how do you go about learning new words and their meanings?

A. Identifying new vocabulary

When you read strictly for pleasure, such as when you read a novel, you usually don't worry about new vocabulary. If you come to a word you don't know, you simply continue reading and you figure out what the author intended by the context. It is not essential that you understand the meaning exactly as long as you understand the passage as a whole. This is often not the case when you read a textbook. Identifying, understanding, and applying new vocabulary is often critical when reading a textbook. Following are some ways that you can identify and understand words that are new to you.

1. Use phonics to sound out the word

Using phonics involves determining the sound of a word by making the sounds represented by each letter or letter group in the word. It is a good idea to try to sound out a word phonetically, especially if you were taught to read using phonics when you were a child. Unfortunately, the English language does not provide phonetics rules that can be applied to every word. Some students—and even adults—have a large vocabulary of words that they simply haven't heard in conversation or elsewhere. Phonics skills can be the link between a vocabulary acquired by hearing and vocabulary learned through reading. Using phonics may also help you to spell words more easily.

2. Use context clues to derive meaning

Many times you can figure out what a word means by observing how it is used in the sentence or paragraph. What part of speech is the unfamiliar word? You may not realize that if you can't figure out the meaning of the word, then you may not understand the passage very well. When this happens, you should look it up in order to make sure that you understand the passage.

3. Use resources such as a glossary or a dictionary

Does the textbook have a glossary? A glossary is a listing, sometimes found in the back of a textbook and sometimes found at the end of a chapter in the book, which provides definitions for words or concepts that the author feels are important to the particular discipline the textbook covers. Sometimes information in the glossary can help you better understand the point of a passage where a glossary word has been used. Dictionaries of various types are also a great resource for college students.

B. Learning new words and definitions

While understanding is always your primary goal, you may discover some discipline-specific vocabulary that you will need to memorize. One strategy to use in these cases would be to make word cards (sometimes called flash cards) that you can use to test yourself. Standard three-by-five-inch index cards are ideal for this activity. Write the vocabulary word or concept on one side of the card and the definition on the opposite side. Test yourself by reading the word and then, without looking at the definition, reciting the definition aloud. Then turn the card over to see if you were correct. If you were correct, go to the next card. If you were incorrect, recite the word and read the correct definition aloud to help fix it in your memory.

Figure 4.1 Example of a Flash Card

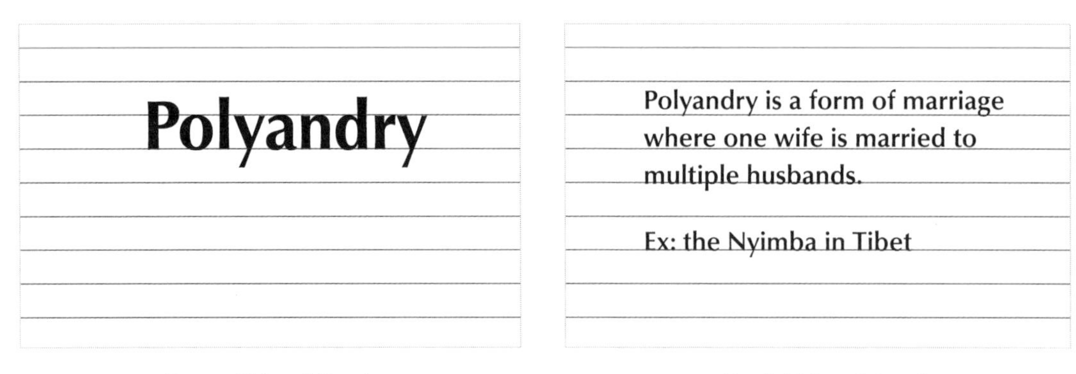

C. *Moving beyond definitions to associations*

It is usually not enough to simply memorize the definitions for new words; you need to understand how these terms relate to other terms and to larger concepts. One strategy that may help you do this is called *concept mapping*.

Concept mapping[13] involves drawing a diagram of the terms to show the relationships between them. For example, if you encountered new vocabulary when reading about different types of marriage, you might draw a concept map like the one illustrated in Figure 4.2. The diagram helps you to easily recognize the ways in which the terms are similar and the ways in which they are different. Monogamy and polygamy are different types of marriage. Strict monogamy and serial monogamy are different types of monogamy. Polygyny and polyandry are different types of polygamy.

Other types of visual organizers include tables, charts, graphs, timelines, flowcharts, diagrams, and webs. Examples of these may be found online.

Figure 4.2 Example of a Concept Map

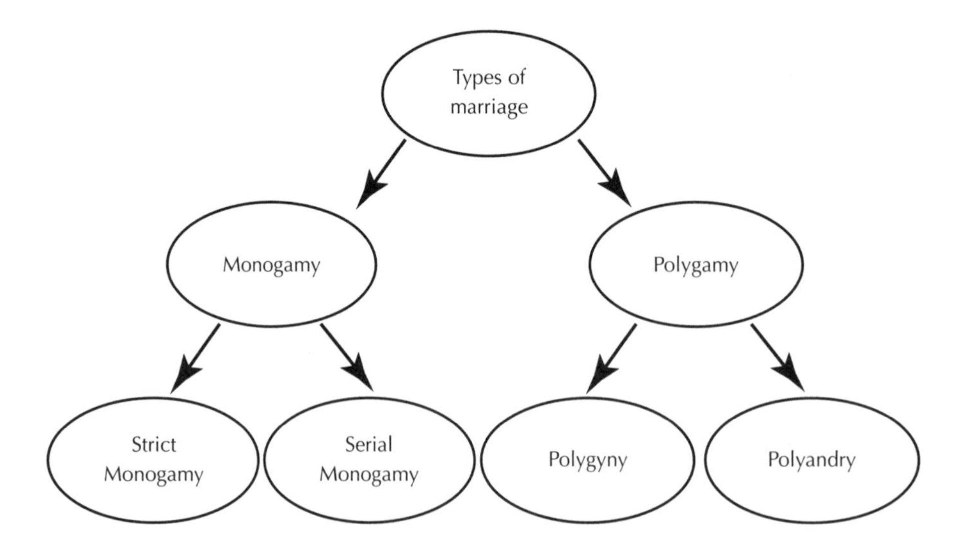

Reading Comprehension Question 4.4 (Analysis)

Which of the following statements is accurate according to this chapter?

a. Reading involves writing.

b. Reading involves asking questions.

c. Reading involves testing yourself.

d. Reading involves distinguishing what information is important.

e. All of these are correct.

Want to learn more? Try these resources.

A table called *Graphing Various Types of Conceptual Relationships* is presented online at the following URL:
http://bvtlab.com/nmsXj

In addition, examples of five different types of visual organizers are presented at the following URL:
http://bvtlab.com/8srAc

SUMMARY

In this chapter you learned why obtaining and reading the textbook in college is so important, as well as how to read a textbook effectively. Proven reading and learning strategies were described in this chapter, including the SOAR (select, organize, associate, and regulate) method and the SQ3R (Survey, Question, Read, Review, and Recite) method. Good and bad attitudes toward reading in college were compared. The section on reading road signs explained ways to vary your reading rate and technique so that it matches the difficulty level and writing style of the passage. Methods for dealing with new vocabulary were identified including using phonics, using context clues, or other resources (a glossary or a dictionary). The chapter also offered techniques for learning new terms and concepts and for making associations between them.

Review Questions 4.1

Instructions: Following are five true-false statements taken from the information in this chapter. First, try to answer them without looking back at the chapter. Then review the chapter to see how well you did.

Question & Answer	Rationale
Circle true or false for each of the following statements.	**Write an explanation stating why each statement is true or false.**
1. A student can be successful in college without buying textbooks. **True or False**	Your Rationale:
2. The SOAR method is good for students who don't have a strategy for reading and study, but students who already have a strategy will most likely perform better if they stick to their own personal strategy because they are most comfortable with it. **True or False**	Your Rationale:
3. Memorizing new vocabulary is necessary, but understanding will always be your primary goal. **True or False**	Your Rationale:
4. Concept maps are a strategy that is designed to help you memorize new vocabulary. **True or False**	Your Rationale:
5. Not understanding words in the textbook is a sign that the student does not have much education. **True or False**	Your Rationale:

Name: ____________________________________

Chapter Four

Study Guide

Chapter 4, Goal 1: The student will be able to explain why reading textbooks in college is so important.

Questions	Answers & Notes

Name: ______________________________

Chapter Four **Study Guide**

Chapter 4, Goal 2: The student will be able to demonstrate how to use a textbook effectively.

Questions	Answers & Notes

Name: ______________________________

Chapter Four **Study Guide**

Chapter 4, Goal 3: The student will be able to describe strategies that can improve reading comprehension.

Questions	Answers & Notes

Name: ______________________________

Chapter Four

Study Guide

Chapter 4, Goal 4: The student will be able to demonstrate the practice of (S) selecting important information from less important information when reading, (O) organizing the information in new ways, (A) associating or creating meaningful connections between ideas, and (R) regulating through practice and self-evaluation.

Questions	Answers & Notes

Name: ______________________________

Chapter Four

Study Guide

Chapter 4, Goal 5: The student will be able to apply the SQ3R method when reading a passage from a text.

Questions	Answers & Notes

Name: ___________________________________

Chapter Four

Study Guide

Chapter 4, Goal 6: The student will be able to use concept mapping as a way to move beyond definitions to associations when learning new vocabulary.

Questions	Answers & Notes

Name: ______________________________

Preparing for Class:
Use This Page to Record Questions or Insights to Discuss in Class.

Practice Identifying New Vocabulary

Goal:

The purpose of this activity is to help students to use and identify new vocabulary in order to read more effectively and to value this activity as a means of gaining greater understanding of what they read.

Objective:

The student will analyze a reading passage from a college level textbook to identify new vocabulary, and then use multiple techniques to understand the vocabulary and gain greater understanding of the passage.

Instructions:

Get a highlighter. Then pick a chapter in one of your textbooks and start reading. As you read, each time you come to a word that you don't know, highlight that word but don't stop reading. Keep going until you have read a few pages. Then use the analysis questions in the following table to think about the words you have identified. Write notes about each question and what you learned in the space provided.

Analysis	Notes
How many words did you highlight?	
Think about each word. Were you able to figure out the meaning for some of the highlighted words just by considering the context of the passages around it? How many of them could you figure out that way?	
Look a few of them up to see if the meaning you have assumed, based on the context, is correct. Did you get them all correct, or were there some that you misunderstood?	
Now look at the remaining highlighted words. How many of the highlighted words are left for which you were not able to figure out the meaning just from context? Look up the definitions of those words in the glossary (or if no glossary is available, use a dictionary). Do you understand the chapter better now that you know the definitions for those words?	
How many of those highlighted words would you consider "important" for this class? Do you think that looking them up will help you score a higher grade on the exams in this class than you would have otherwise?	

Chapter 5 Roadmap

Focus on Learning: Why Am I Really in College?

In this chapter you will learn about the types of attitudes and approaches to learning that help make students successful.

This chapter roadmap page presents the formal learning goals for this chapter and a checklist that you should follow as you read and study the chapter.

Student Learning Goals for This Chapter

After completing this chapter you should be able to do the following:

1. Compare and contrast the focus-on-grades approach with the focus-on-learning approach.
2. Explain why the focus-on-learning approach is most effective.
3. Explain why long-term learning is more productive than cramming for an exam.
4. Describe the characteristics of a responsible learner.
5. Explain how failure to take responsibility for learning—both on the part of students and on the part of professors—can be detrimental to both individuals and society.
6. Explain the difference between deep learning and surface learning.

Checklist for This Chapter

Target date/ deadline	Check when completed	Activity
________	❑	1. Complete Critical Thinking Activity 5.1.
________	❑	2. Convert the learning goals above to questions that you can answer as you read the chapter. Write your questions on the study guide pages near the end of this chapter.
________	❑	3. Read the chapter.
________	❑	4. Try to answer the reading comprehension questions as you come to them in the chapter. Check each answer by comparing it to the list of correct answers in the back of the book. If any answer was not correct, then review the passages preceding the question to see why you missed the question.
________	❑	5. Use the study guide pages near the end of this chapter to write down the answers to the questions you created in Step 2. Once completed, these pages will be your study guide.
________	❑	6. Write down any questions, insights, or comments that you have as you read so that you can bring them up in class (if applicable).
________	❑	7. Complete Review Questions 5.1.
________	❑	8. Complete Assignment 5.1 (Form a study group).

CRITICAL THINKING ACTIVITY 5.1

Consider the following questions; select the answer that most closely matches your personal preference for each situation described.

1. You have been rushed to the hospital after an auto accident. Which would you prefer?

   a. To be treated by a nurse who earned her credentials by cheating on the final exam in nursing school

   b. To be treated by a nurse who, thanks to her excellent negotiating skills, was able to graduate nursing school by bargaining with the professor after failing a final the exam

   c. To be treated by a nurse who earned her credentials, not only by learning enough to pass her exams, but also by making sure that she understood everything that she was supposed to learn

2. You are an elementary school principal who is interviewing applicants to teach a second grade class at your school. Your child is in that second grade class. Which would you prefer?

   a. To hire an applicant who passed her math class by taking the class online and having a friend who was good at math take all of the exams for her

   b. To hire an applicant who says in the interview, "I only want to teach at the first, second, or third grade levels because I don't like math"

   c. To hire an applicant who struggled with math initially, but who passed the class because she spent extra time doing practice questions and getting help from the tutoring lab until she mastered the subject

3. You have won the lottery and are now 100 million dollars richer than you were yesterday. You don't know how to properly manage this large amount of money or how to deal with the tax issues associated with it, so you decide to hire a CPA to help you. Which would you prefer?

   a. To have your finances managed by an accountant who earned his credentials by cheating on the final exam in college

   b. To have your finances managed by an accountant who believes in investing as little effort as possible to get the most benefit possible (When he was in college he used ratemyprofessor.com to figure out which professors were easy and took only easy classes. This way he was able to get his degree without having to invest very much time in studying or learning.)

   c. To have your finances managed by an accountant who is good at his job because when he was in college he took responsibility for his own learning and researched topics deeply until he gained a clear understanding of everything he needed to know to earn his degree and to do his job well

Is there a pattern to your answers for these three questions? If so, why? Make some notes on the next page about what you think, and be prepared to discuss this in class.

Focus on Learning:
Why Am I Really in College?

Learn as if you will live forever; live as if you will die tomorrow.

— *Gandhi*[1]

While grading an essay, an English professor noticed that the student author had obviously not taken the time to proofread before submitting the paper. With a quiet sigh of disappointment, the professor marked the freshman paper with a C (average) and then inserted a small note in the margin which read, "Is this your best work?" Years later, at the retirement dinner for the English professor, the president of the college stood to make a few remarks and read from a letter that he had recently received from one of the professor's former students. The letter of gratitude recounted that moment when the professor had written "Is this your best work?" on a poorly written essay. In the letter, the former student explained, "Those words changed my life." Inspired by those words, the student decided never to take a mediocre approach to learning again. The student began to apply an above-average effort and to produce above-average work. The student eventually graduated with honors.

In this chapter you will learn about the attitudes and approaches to learning that help make students successful. The proper attitude and approach to college learning can convert the average student into an exceptional one. You will learn to develop a focus on learning instead of a focus on grades, to be a responsible learner, to use learning goals as a guide to studying, to engage in deep learning instead of surface learning, and to distribute your study workload over the entire semester instead of cramming the night before for exams. These principles will help you to do your best work.

In the pages that follow, this chapter examines the student's approach to learning with regard to focus, goals, pace, depth, and responsibility.

5.1 Focus

Most students have been socialized to view the acquisition of a credential as the paramount purpose for college, and therefore they focus on grades rather than on learning. However, the focus-on-grades approach is not as effective in reaching the desired educational outcomes as is the focus-on-learning approach. Figure 5.1 illustrates this point.

Students who employ a focus-on-grades approach will naturally learn less than they could because they are likely to think of the grade as something separate from learning. Given this focus, students attempt to achieve the desired grades with the least investment possible—such that the driving question becomes, "What is the least (time, learning, effort, etc.) I can invest and still pass?" Some students who employ this focus on least effort may be satisfied if the result is a passing grade because that grade will not prevent them from acquiring a credential. However, this model may prevent them from acquiring the level of true learning of which they are capable. In fact, a focus on grades may result in very little true learning. True learning is distinguished from the type of short-term learning that is produced by cramming for exams.

In contrast, students who focus on learning as the goal will seek to learn as much as they can. They are more likely to embrace, "What is the most I can learn?" as their driving question. In this case, higher grades will be an automatic result (a side effect) of greater learning. These students will earn a credential, and they will also experience a greater degree of true learning with long-term benefits. They may also achieve a higher grade point average since true learning equips them to earn higher grades.

Figure 5.1 Two Approaches: Comparison of a Focus on Grades with a Focus on Learning

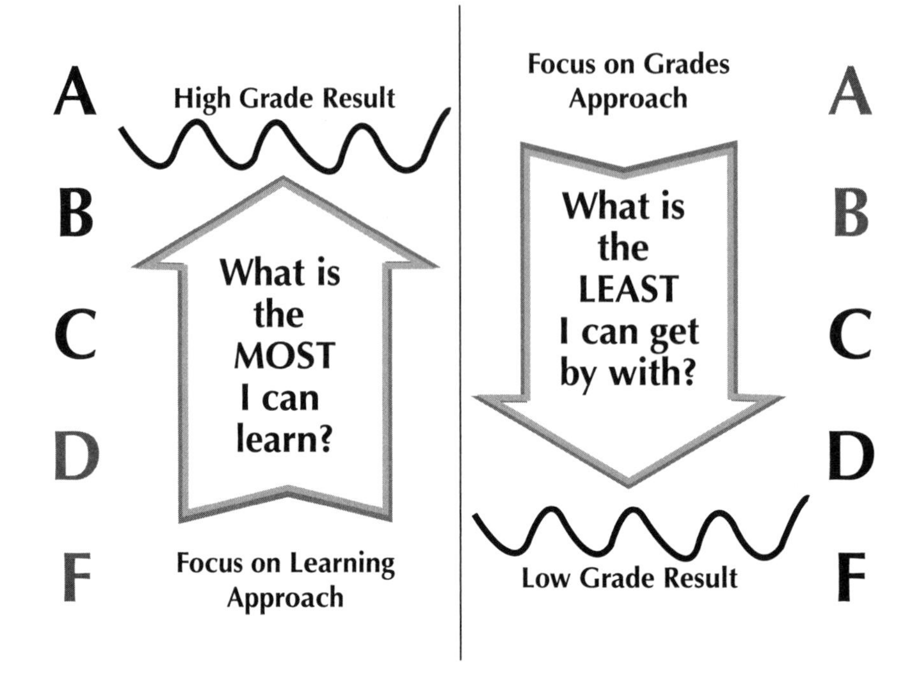

Table 5.1 Contrasting Questions Associated with Academic Focus

Focus on Grades	Focus on Learning
What is the least I can do to pass this course?	What is the most that I can learn in this class?
What will be on the test?	What are the lesson objectives?
What do I have to memorize?	What am I supposed to learn?
What shortcuts can I use to prepare for the exam?	What can I do to best learn the important material in this lesson?

Consider the questions listed in Table 5.1. Which focus describes your approach to learning in college? You will be more successful if you focus on learning because higher grades are automatically a result of better learning. The best way to score highly on exams is simply to learn the lesson. Don't settle for a focus-on-grades approach because that approach results in less learning, and as a consequence, lower grades. After all, if you are going to invest years of your life in going to college, don't you want to get more than just grades for your investment of time? You deserve more. You deserve an education, rather than just a credential, because once you truly learn something no one can ever take that away from you.

5.2 Goals

As T. A. Angelo noted, "When learners know what their educational goals are and figure out how they can best achieve them [and when they] know how and how well their goals fit the instructor's, they tend to learn more and get better grades." Researchers and educational experts have found that goal alignment between teacher and student is key to learning success.[2] Therefore, students will be more successful when they identify the learning goals or objectives for each course, lesson, or exam and incorporate them into their study routine.

Even if you adopt a focus-on-learning approach, you can't learn everything in one semester or course. Therefore, in order to be successful in each course, you will need to identify the goals for that course. The course goals are usually listed in the syllabus. They are usually somewhat broad because they apply to the entire course. Some professors also publish learning objectives (objectives are more specific than goals, and are measurable) for chapters, lessons, or exams within a course. Sometimes chapter objectives are listed in the textbook. Lesson objectives make an excellent guide for you to use when you design your study plan. Your focus should remain on learning as much as you can; however, with the addition of specific measurable lesson objectives, **you will know what you are supposed to learn**—and you will have a way to assess what you have learned.

Lesson objectives simply state the desired outcome of the lesson. In other words, they state what the student should be able to do after completing the lesson. Instead of the term "objectives," we could call them the "intended learning outcomes"[3] because they state what you should be able to do after learning that you could not do before. A typical lesson objective may begin, "Upon completion of this lesson, the student will be able to ..." followed by a specific type of knowledge, analysis, skill, or behavior. Following are some examples of different types of learning goals based on Bloom's Taxonomy:[4]

> Knowledge Goal: Upon completion of this lesson, the student will be able to list and describe the characteristics of a mammal.
>
> Application/Analysis Goal: Upon completion of this lesson, the student will be able to compare and contrast a democratic society and a communist society.
>
> Application/Skill Goal: Upon completion of this lesson, the student will be able to perform CPR on an infant and demonstrate this skill using the first aid dummies.
>
> Behavior Goal: Upon completion of this lesson, the student will design and implement a three-week personal weight-training program to strengthen gross motor muscles.

Since the objectives are usually presented as statements of outcome rather than as questions, it may be useful for you (the student) to convert the objectives into one or more questions that can be used as a study guide. For example, the first learning goal for this chapter can be converted into at least five questions (see Table 5.2). Once you have created your own questions based on the professor's objectives, you should identify information relating to those questions as you read the chapter, and attempt to answer them afterwards. If you have difficulty answering any of the questions on your own, you can bring them up during class discussion or ask for help outside of class. Professors set aside office hours specifically for the purpose of helping their students with such questions.

You may recall from Chapter 1 that one of the differences between high school and college is that in college, professors schedule regular office hours in order to meet with students individually. Scheduled office hours are usually posted in the syllabus, on the professor's website, and on the office door. As Chapter 1 already noted, you are not interrupting or bothering professors when you meet with them during their office hours. That time has been set aside especially for you. In fact, professors are often impressed by students who take the initiative to write down a question about the reading or lesson and to ask about that question during an office hour visit. So when you have questions about the lesson that are not answered by the reading, lecture, or class discussion, make an appointment to see the professor during office hours. **It is important that you close any gaps between what you have learned so far and what you are supposed to learn.**

Table 5.2 | Example of Study Guide Questions Based on a Lesson Objective

Objective:	Upon completion of this lesson, the student will be able to compare and contrast the focus-on-grades approach with the focus-on-learning approach and explain why the focus-on-learning approach is more effective.
Questions:	1. What is the focus-on-grades approach?
	2. What is the focus-on-learning approach?
	3. In what ways are the two approaches, focus-on-grades and focus-on-learning, similar?
	4. In what ways are the two approaches different?
	5. In what ways is the focus-on-learning approach more effective than the focus-on-grades approach?

If neither your professor nor the textbook provides lesson objectives or exam objectives, then you may wish to inquire about them. In the absence of having objectives provided, you will need to create your own list of objectives in order to organize your study regimen.

Reading Comprehension Question 5.1 (Knowledge)

Researchers and educational experts have found which of the following?

a. That goal alignment between the teacher and the student is key to learning success
b. That goals are not a significant part of the educational process
c. That goals cause students to focus on grades and not on learning
d. That students who have goals tend to get bogged down and not learn as much as those who do not have goals

5.3 Pace

Many students wait, incorrectly, until the night before an exam (or a day or two before) to begin studying the material that will be covered. This is famously known as "cramming" for the exam. It is a strategy that may have worked in high school, when less material was covered on a single exam, but it is much less effective in college. Many college courses have only two exams—a midterm and a final—and sometimes the final is cumulative (covering everything taught in the course). Therefore, the student must master a large amount of information in order to perform well on each exam.

Researchers have discovered that *how you study* is more important than *how long you study*.[5] Students who spread out their study time over days and weeks score higher grades than students who study the same number of hours all in one night.

Michaels and Miethe examined more than fifteen variables including study habits and performance for 676 undergraduate college students. They explained the difference that they found between crammers and non-crammers:

> The return of study time and class attendance on grades varies by type of study habits. Among students who study throughout the week (non-crammers), both study time and class attendance have significant positive effects on grades. For crammers, the amounts of study and class attendance have no appreciable effect on college grades. In other words, students who study throughout the week benefit from increased study time and class attendance, whereas students who concentrate their studying before exams do not reap rewards from increases in effort.[5]

One problem with cramming is that it relies on short-term memory. It is difficult, if not impossible, to hold as much information in your short-term memory as is often required on college-level exams (especially comprehensive final exams). The key is to study on a regular basis and *learn* the material a little bit at a time. This method will allow you to encode the course material in your long-term memory, which will serve you well when you take the exam.[6] In fact, some researchers[7] have found that students who reported that they used cramming "for most of their courses" tended to have lower GPAs.

One key to success in learning is to pace yourself. Design a study plan for each course in which you anticipate what you need to learn for each exam, and then divide that huge block of learning into a number of study sessions. Learning the information in smaller sessions spread out over time will enable you to engage in deeper learning.

5.4 Depth

Do you have high expectations for yourself? Are you doing your best work? One way to do your best work is to employ deep learning instead of surface learning.

Learning has been defined as "an active, interactive, self-aware process that results in meaningful, long-lasting changes in knowledge, skills, behaviors, beliefs, and attitudes ... that cannot be attributed primarily to maturation."[2] But not all learning is of the same quality. It is useful to distinguish between deep learning and surface learning.

Surface learning is often employed by those who cram for an exam. It involves very limited thinking, analysis, or critical evaluation. Surface learners often separate new material from the context in which they find it, and as a result they have little ability to apply what they have learned to a real-world context. For example, a student who uses surface learning techniques to study for an exam might simply try to memorize the definitions of all the words printed in **bold** in the textbook. Memorization is not always a bad technique—but when words are memorized out of context, the student is often unable to apply the terms that he or she has memorized because the terms are not fully understood.

Deep learning involves critical thinking and the analysis of new information with the goal of understanding the concepts and acquiring the ability to apply them in different contexts. In deep learning, the student intends to move beyond simple memorization to understanding and application.

You may use the information in Table 5.3 to compare the deep-learning approach with the surface-learning approach. These characteristics have been described by Entwistle[8] and presented by Norton.[9]

Reading Comprehension Question 5.2 (Literal Comprehension)

Which of the following is the main difference between deep learning and surface learning?

a. Surface learning is often used by students who study over several weeks for exams.

b. Deep learning involves critical thinking and analysis of new information.

c. Deep learning tends to distract students from the main goal of the course.

d. Surface learning can help the student learn a lot of information in a very short time.

Table 5.3 Comparison of Deep Learning and Surface Learning

Characteristic	Deep Approach	Surface Approach
Intent of Student	Intends to understand	Intends to complete task requirements
Mode of study	Interacts vigorously with content	Memorizes information needed for assessments
Level of understanding	Relates new ideas to previous knowledge	Fails to distinguish principles from examples
Application of concepts	Relates concepts to everyday experience	Treats task as an external imposition
Integration of concepts	Relates evidence to conclusions	Focuses on discrete elements without integration
Level of critical thinking	Examines the logic of the argument	Neglects to reflect on purpose or strategies

It is important to note that "these approaches [are] not personality traits or intellectual abilities of any kind; *they are simply a reflection of the student's intention* when s/he engages in a given academic task."[9] It may be the case that some students are unaware of the difference between deep and surface learning. Such students may wrongly assume that surface learning is the normal approach taken by everyone. Therefore, now that you are aware of this dynamic, you can adjust your intent and embrace the more effective deep-learning approach. The surface approach nearly always leads to poorer quality outcomes[10] while the deep approach can lead to clear understanding, long-term recall, and higher grades.

Want to learn more?

Try these resources.

View the You Tube video depicting *Surface Learning vs. Deep Learning* at the following URLs (The videos summarize concepts developed by John Biggs in his book, *Teaching for Quality Learning at University*):
Part 1: http://bvtlab.com/4n8m8
Part 2: http://bvtlab.com/9E77W
Part 3: http://bvtlab.com/67n79

Think About This:

What would be different about the way you read a typical textbook (such as history or sociology) if you used a deep approach rather than a surface approach?

5.5 Responsibility

College is an environment where adult students—who already have a foundation of basic academic skills—come together under the guidance of the professor to learn and engage in higher level **critical thinking** about a wide range of subjects that will prepare them for leadership roles in society. As a college student you must take adult responsibility for your own learning. Taking adult responsibility means that you do not wait for the teacher to tell you what to do or what to think, or to ask you questions. Instead you ask questions, design a study plan for your classes, and reach out to the professor and your classmates for assistance in the learning process. Learning is not something that someone else does for you or makes you do. Learning is something you do for yourself with the assistance of your mentors and peers.

"Learning takes place through the active behavior of the student: it is what he does that he learns, not what the teacher does."

— *Ralph W. Tyler*[11]

Responsible adult learners do not need to be told to read the syllabus, acquire a textbook, read the textbook, develop a study regimen, prepare questions in advance to use in class participation, attend class and other academic functions on campus, participate, keep up their grades, evaluate their own progress on a regular basis, plan for early registration in advance, consult their advisor, or seek help when they need it (long before an exam). Responsible students take the initiative to do all of these things and more, not because they wish to please the professor, but because they wish to gain as much from the educational experience as they can.

Responsible adult students do not whine about their grades and beg for points that they have not earned. Instead, they view low grades as a signal that they have not been learning well enough in that class; and they respond by adjusting their study habits, getting help, or making other changes that will enable them to learn more effectively. Assessing yourself and making changes to promote greater learning will naturally result in higher grades.

Georgia Tech professor and physicist, Dr. Kurt Wiesenfield, authored an article in *Newsweek* called "Making the Grade: Many Students Wheedle for a Degree as if It Were a Freebie T-Shirt" in which he underscored how important it is for students to take responsibility for learning in order to become competent leaders in society.[12]

Professor Wiesenfield tells the story of how twelve students called him after the semester was completely over in order to beg him to change their failing grades. One student cried, "I will lose my scholarship if you don't change my grade to a D," while another whined "If you don't give me a C, I'll flunk out." One student dramatically pleaded, "If I don't pass, my life is over."[7] The professor was alarmed that these students were so indifferent toward grades as an indication of personal effort and performance. As he explained,

> Many, when pressed about why they think they deserve a better grade, admit they don't. Having been raised on gold stars for effort and smiley faces for self-esteem, they've learned that they can get by without hard work and real talent if they can talk the professor into giving them a break. … Their arguments for wheedling better grades often ignore academic performance. … Perhaps these students see me as a commodities broker with something they want—a grade. Though intrinsically worthless, grades, if properly manipulated, can be traded for what has value: a degree, which means a job, which means money. The one thing college actually offers—a chance to learn—is considered irrelevant, even less than worthless, because of the long hours and hard work required.[12]

It appears that focusing on grades and shortcuts, instead of on learning, had very serious negative consequences for these physics students. Perhaps some of them lost their scholarships, perhaps some failed and had to change majors, and perhaps some allowed their GPA to drop so low that they were never able to graduate.

However, Professor Wiesenfield explains that there would also be dire consequences for our entire society if he were to award these students passing grades that they did not deserve:

> These guys had better take themselves seriously now, because our country will be forced to take them seriously later, when the stakes are much higher. They must recognize that their attitude is not only self-destructive, but socially destructive. The erosion of quality control—giving

appropriate grades for actual accomplishments—is a major concern ... That's when the misfortunes of eroding academic standards multiply. We lament that school children get "kicked upstairs" until they graduate from high school despite being illiterate and mathematically inept, but we seem unconcerned with college graduates whose less blatant deficiencies are far more harmful if their accreditation exceeds their qualifications. Most of my students are science and engineering majors. If they're good at getting partial credit but not at getting the answer right, then the new bridge breaks or the new drug doesn't work. One finds examples here in Atlanta. ... a light tower in the Olympic Stadium collapsed killing a worker. ... showing real-world consequences of errors and lack of expertise.[12]

Want to learn more? Try these resources.

You can read Professor Wiesenfield's entire article online at any one of the following URLs:

http://bvtlab.com/p6g7q
http://bvtlab.com/8gbbp
http://bvtlab.com/a78ec
http://bvtlab.com/p6u7B

Think About This:

What was Professor Wiesenfield's main message in this article?

Why is Professor Wiesenfield opposed to grade inflation?

How could Professor Wiesenfield's students have avoided this tragedy?

Reading Comprehension Question 5.3 (Inferential Comprehension)

What was Professor Wiesenfield's main point in the above article?

a. That some of his students would be in trouble in the real world because they had an attitude about learning that was not appropriate for a college education

b. That some of his students asked for grades they did not deserve

c. That all students are trying to get away with the least amount of work possible in college

d. None of the above

Summary

In this chapter you learned how the proper attitude and approach to college learning can help you be successful. Successful students focus on learning and ask, "What is the most that I can learn in this class?" Successful students identify the learning goals or objectives for each course, lesson, or exam and incorporate them into their study routine. For each course, successful students design a study plan in which they divide the learning activities into a number of study sessions spread out over time. Successful students practice a deep-learning approach instead of a surface-learning approach. Successful students take adult responsibility for their learning.

In this book you will learn how to take responsibility for your own learning. This starts with identifying and practicing successful learning approaches. Specific academic skills and habits will be covered in the coming chapters.

Reading Comprehension Question 5.4 (Analysis)

Why did the authors write this chapter on "Focus on Learning"?

a. To enlighten the student on how to approach the topic of learning in a college atmosphere

b. To chide the student on his/her behavior in college

c. To show that students are always trying to get away with the least amount of work

d. To demonstrate that learning is almost impossible in a college setting

Review Questions 5.1

Instructions: Following are five true-false statements taken from the information in this chapter. First, try to answer them without looking back at the chapter. Then review the chapter to see how well you did.

Question & Answer	Rationale
Circle True or False for each of the following.	**Write an explanation stating why each statement is true or false.**
1. Cramming for exams is a normal part of college life for most students because it is the best way to learn the large volume of material covered in most college courses. **True or False**	Your Rationale:
2. A successful approach to studying and learning demands a focus on grades because college students must maintain a certain grade point average (GPA) in order to graduate. **True or False**	Your Rationale:
3. The surface approach to learning nearly always leads to poorer outcomes and/or lower grades. **True or False**	Your Rationale:
4. The focus-on-grades model is a failure model. **True or False**	Your Rationale:
5. "Wheedle" is the nickname or label that Professor Wiesenfield has applied to students who try to pass the course by cheating. **True or False**	Your Rationale:

Name: ______________________________

Chapter Five

Study Guide

Chapter 5, Goal 1: The student will be able to compare and contrast the focus-on-grades approach with the focus-on-learning approach.

Questions	Answers & Notes

Name: ____________________________

Chapter Five | Study Guide

Chapter 5, Goal 2: The student will be able to explain why the focus-on-learning approach is most effective.

Questions	Answers & Notes

Name: ______________________________

Chapter Five

Study Guide

Chapter 5, Goal 3: The student will be able to explain why long-term learning is more productive than cramming for an exam.

Questions	Answers & Notes

Name: ____________________________________

Chapter Five

Study Guide

Chapter 5, Goal 4: The student will be able to describe the characteristics of a responsible learner.

Questions	Answers & Notes

Name: ______________________

Chapter Five

Study Guide

Chapter 5, Goal 5: The student will be able to explain how failure to take responsibility for learning—on the part of students and professors—can be detrimental to both individuals and society.

Questions	Answers & Notes

Name: ______________________________

Chapter Five

Study Guide

Chapter 5, Goal 6: The student will be able to explain the difference between deep learning and surface learning.

Questions	Answers & Notes

Name: ________________________________

Preparing for Class:
Use This Page to Record Questions or Insights to Discuss in Class.

Study Group (2–4 people for four meetings)

Goal:

The purpose of this activity is to enable the student to use study groups to learn more effectively.

Objective:

The student will form or join a study group for one of his or her classes and will keep a record of his or her study group involvement and activities.

Instructions:

It is smart to study with other students who are taking the same course and who are serious about learning.

Follow these steps to benefit from being in a study group for one of your classes:

Step 1: Consult one or more of the following websites to learn about the value of study groups and how to use them effectively:

Study Groups and College Success from the University of LaVerne, Learning Center **(http://bvtlab.com/3wFr6)**

BookRags Article: *How to Form a Study Group in College* **(http://bvtlab.com/h5dPe)**

Peer Study Groups from the University of Michigan **(http://bvtlab.com/8W7v7)**

Step 2: Form a group and hold at least four study sessions together. Record the following for each group study session: 1) the date, time, and place of the group meeting; 2) the signatures of all who attended; and 3) a brief description of what the group did during that session.

Step 3: You can use the Study Group Report Form on the next page to keep a record of your group meetings.

Study Group Report Form

Course:	Your Name:
First Meeting What did the group do at this meeting?	Date: ____________________ Attendees' Signatures
Second Meeting What did the group do at this meeting?	Date: ____________________ Attendees' Signatures
Third Meeting What did the group do at this meeting?	Date: ____________________ Attendees' Signatures
Fourth Meeting What did the group do at this meeting?	Date: ____________________ Attendees' Signatures

Chapter 6 Roadmap

Learning Styles: How Do I Learn Best?

In this chapter you will examine learning style preferences and study strategies associated with each style that can help you learn more effectively. The goal of this chapter is to help you to become more aware of your personal learning preferences and to provide some tips for how you, individually, can learn best.

This chapter roadmap page presents the formal learning goals for this chapter and a checklist that you should follow as you read and study the chapter.

Student Learning Goals for This Chapter

After completing this chapter the student should be able to do the following:

1. Describe eight types of learners and learning styles.
2. Analyze your own personal learning preferences using the *Index of Learning Styles (ILS)*.
3. List at least two study strategies that will help you learn more effectively based on your learning style.

Checklist for This Chapter

Target date/ deadline	Check when completed	Activity
________	❑	1. Complete Critical Thinking Activity 6.1.
________	❑	2. Convert the learning goals above to questions that you can answer as you read the chapter. Write your questions on the study guide pages near the end of this chapter.
________	❑	3. Read the chapter.
________	❑	4. Try to answer the reading comprehension questions as you come to them in the chapter. Check each answer by comparing it to the list of correct answers in the back of the book. If any answer was not correct, then review the passages preceding the question to see why you missed the question.
________	❑	5. Use the study guide pages near the end of this chapter to write down the answers to the questions you created in Step 2. Once completed, these pages will be your study guide.
________	❑	6. Write down any questions, insights, or comments that you have as you read so that you can bring them up in class (if applicable).
________	❑	7. Complete Review Questions 6.1.
________	❑	8. Complete Assignment 6.1 (Discover Your Learning Styles).

CRITICAL THINKING ACTIVITY 6.1

As a way to begin thinking about the topic of this chapter, please consider the following questions and write your answers in the space provided.

For a moment, think about how you learn. Consider a time when you felt that you were learning, and also consider a time when you wanted to learn but found it very difficult. In either of those cases, was there something specific you did to try to make learning easier or more pleasant? If so, did it work? What was the outcome?

Have there been times when you were really excited about learning something new?

When was that? What was the topic? Was it an active or passive project?

Learning Styles:

How Do I Learn Best?

"

What is important is to keep learning, to enjoy challenge, and to tolerate ambiguity.
In the end, there are no certain answers.

— *Martina Horner, President of Radcliffe College*[1]

"

You might have already noticed that you tend to learn in certain ways no matter what class you are taking. In high school, you may have noticed that some of your teachers delivered material in a way that made it easy for you to learn and to remember, while in other classes the material seemed difficult to learn and to retain. This is because we each have our own unique way of receiving and cataloguing information, and faculty members also have their own unique ways of imparting their knowledge and information about their specialty area.

If your learning style happens to match your professor's teaching style, you may find it easy to remember information from lectures and classes. If your learning style doesn't match his or her teaching style, however, you may find yourself saying, "I just can't learn in this class; I must be bad at this subject," or "I just can't seem to understand what this professor is trying to teach me." Most students have had the uncomfortable experience of feeling that they "just can't learn" something that is important to them.

To maximize your success in college, it will help if you can identify your own personal learning preferences; then *you* can take specific actions that might help you to learn even when your style and your professor's style do not match. Helping you to do this is a goal of this chapter.

Reading Comprehension Question 6.1 (Knowledge)

Which of the following best describes the goal of this chapter?

a. To help you to become more aware of your personal learning preferences and to provide some tips for how you can best learn
b. To teach you how to learn
c. To explain why learning is important
d. To divide learning up into sections, so it is easier to understand

6.1 Individual Orientation to Learning

The goal of this chapter is to help you to become more aware of your personal learning preferences and to provide some tips for how you can best learn. Since college is a place where your primary activity will be learning, it is important for you to discover that you have a unique style and preference for how you learn.

Up to this point, you may not have given this much thought. Consider the following: when you are presented with new information, what are the ways in which you are most comfortable taking in, making sense of it, and understanding how it relates to the topic at hand?

There has been a great deal of research on the topic of learning. How people learn is of interest to educators of all levels, from kindergarten all the way to college at the post-graduate level. Felder teaches engineering and has studied extensively the learning and teaching styles in engineering education.[2] His research provides great ideas for how students and teachers can work toward creating a better learning environment. In addition, he has developed a well-used measurement tool: the *Index of Learning Styles (ILS)*. We'll use this tool later in the chapter for determining your personal learning style.

If we could discover how each person learns best and then tailor information to meet that person's learning needs, school would surely be a much more user-friendly place. But that is a tall order. In fact, it would be impossible to identify just one specific learning style that a person uses all of the time because we often tailor our learning styles to a particular situation. You have done this throughout your school career, even if you weren't aware of doing so. However, there are preferences that can be measured in people's learning styles, and *your preferences* will help to guide you in your study habits throughout college and life.

As illustrated in Figure 6.1, a person's **orientation to learning** includes three parts: 1) their level of intellectual development, 2) their approach to learning, and 3) their personal learning style. We will explore **learning styles** in this chapter. This chapter includes a presentation of various learning styles, and you will recognize yourself in some of them. Most importantly, you will learn how to measure your own personal learning style and think about study strategies that work best with your style.

Want to learn more?

Try these resources.

If you want to know more about the research and studies regarding learning styles, about how students learn, and about how faculty try to teach to accommodate student learning, you can access the following websites of interest:

Richard Felder's Home Page:
http://bvtlab.com/qU9Yc

Felder and Silverman (1988)
http://bvtlab.com/6Ngk7

Felder and Brent (2005)
http://bvtlab.com/fTuW9

Figure 6.1 Each Person Has Their Own Individual Orientation to Learning

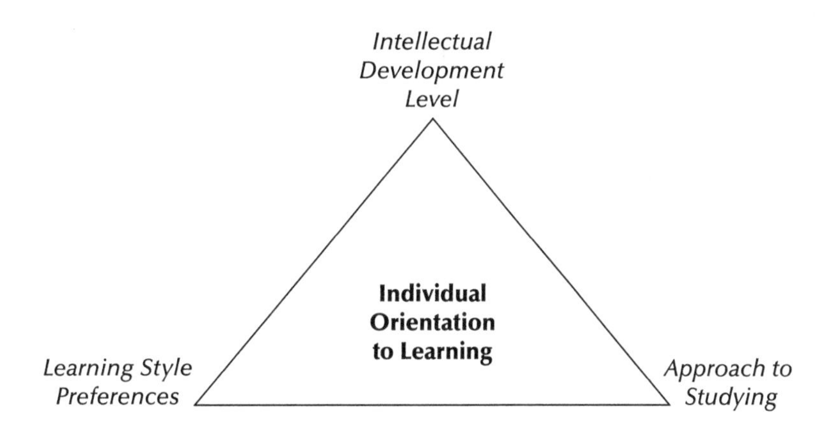

Reading Comprehension Question 6.2 (Literal Comprehension)

Which of the following groups make up an individual's orientation to learning?

a. Each student's approach to studying, intellectual development, and learning style preferences
b. Each student's time spent studying, goals, and courses and outlines for each course
c. Each student's knowledge of a subject, past experience in class, and professors' attitudes
d. None of the above

Reading Comprehension Question 6.3 (Inferential Comprehension)

The main idea of the paragraphs above discussing approaches to learning and Figure 6.1 is which of the following?

a. Each student has an individual approach to learning
b. Each professor can teach his or her students how to learn
c. Each student basically uses a surface approach to learning
d. Each student has an in-depth approach to learning

6.2 Learning Styles and Strategies

Students preferentially take in and process information in different ways: by seeing and hearing, by reflecting and acting, by reasoning logically and intuitively, by analyzing and visualizing, and by progressing steadily and in fits and starts. Teaching methods also vary. Some instructors lecture, while others demonstrate or lead students to self-discovery; some focus on principles and others on applications; and some emphasize memory and others understanding.[3]

There are different learning style preferences that each of us use when we are presented with new information, and that is the topic of this chapter. Your success in college will depend on your self-awareness of your own learning approaches, your knowledge of which approaches you tend to use most often, and your ability to identify when your approach does not match the demands of a course. Exercising flexibility in your approach to match the demands of different courses will help you be more successful.

You probably recognize that there are certain things you do when you study that help you to learn. Have you ever noticed that you study differently when you are trying to learn math compared to English or perhaps psychology? Felder has published much research in the area of learning style preferences.[2] Although there are other theories and ideas about how people learn, for this chapter, we'll focus on the Felder-Silverman model.

The Felder-Silverman model suggests that there are eight types of learners (or eight learning style preferences). They are 1) active learners, 2) reflective learners, 3) sensing learners, 4) intuitive learners, 5) visual learners, 6) verbal learners, 7) global learners, and 8) sequential learners. Table 6.1 describes the different types of learners and offers some tips for studying based on learning style preference. As your read it, keep in mind that each person does not have only one learning style preference. In fact, most of us carry the potential for learning in all the ways that are described in Table 6.1. We tend to use certain types of learning style preferences based on the situation in which we find ourselves. This is to say that you are not locked into a certain learning style preference, but rather you can learn to exercise different styles in different circumstances. Thus, learning style preferences are not traits that we cannot change (such as age, sex, or gender) but are, instead, fluid characteristics that we can alter if we so desire.

Think About This:

Try to recall two classes in which you used totally different study strategies. Think about the topic that you were learning in each class (for example, a science class versus a history class). Think about why you chose the particular study strategy for one of the courses but a different study strategy for the other course.

Do you think the type of study activities that helped you most varied depending on the type of course? Why or why not?

6.3 Discovering Your Own Learning Styles

Richard M. Felder and Barbara A. Soloman of North Carolina State University have developed an *Index of Learning Styles*[4] that can be used to assess preferences on four dimensions (active/reflective, sensing/intuitive, visual/verbal, and sequential/global) of the Felder-Silverman model.[2] The index consists of forty-four simple questions that you can answer for yourself online. Then, when you submit your answers, the computer will display a results' page that shows to what degree you prefer each style. In Assignment 6.1, you will be instructed to browse the *ILS* webpage to complete the index and print your results. The following pages in this section will explain how to interpret your results' page.

Students who want to find out their own learning style profiles and educators who may use the *ILS* for teaching, advising, or research should take into account two important points:

1. The *ILS* results are only one measure of your learning preferences and thus should never be over-interpreted. There are times when you may not agree with the *ILS* interpretation of your preferences. In those cases, you should always trust your own judgment over the results you get with the *ILS*.

2. Your learning style profile gives you a measure of potential strengths and habits, which might cause you problems in academic settings. The profile does not reflect your ability or inability to be successful in a particular subject, discipline, or profession. Labeling students in this way is misleading—and to do so could be destructive if the label is used as justification for a major shift in your career goals or if faculty were to use the label to change curriculum.

Table 6.1 Learning Style Descriptions and Tips for Studying*

Learning Style Preference	Description of Learners	Tips for Studying
Active Learners	• Learn by doing something active with the information—role-playing situations, moving, doing, touching, manipulating, using tools—mostly hands-on techniques • Say, "Let me try this out." • Enjoy working in groups • Enjoy concept demonstrations • Are able to master skills through practice and imitation • Learn well from excursions and field trips • Tend to collect items • Are weak at spelling • Use hands to communicate and talk fast • Are good at sports • Enjoy having music playing in the background while working or studying • Take frequent breaks while studying • Enjoy arts and crafts, science experiments, etc. • Become restless during long lectures • Are able to learn best when they are free to move about • Study often most effectively while lying down, fiddling with objects, etc. • Are often not the best at penmanship • Are often good at playing a musical instrument • Are often good at dance, martial arts • Touch others often in a gesture of friendship	• Study in a group and take turns with explaining concepts to each other, guessing what will be on the next test, and asking each other questions. • Engage in a hands-on activity and try to find ways to do something active with the information you are learning, such as practicing a technique, creating a model that demonstrates the primary concept, etc. • Study in a position that is comfortable, even if it is not a traditional desk or table-and-chair setup, holding the book in your hands. • Take a field trip. • Work on drills or memory exercises or listen to recordings of lectures while walking or exercising. • Mime or act out key points for memory reinforcement. • Try standing up when giving an explanation of something. • Jot down notes while you are reading. • Use beats or rhythm to explain or memorize information. • Sit near the front of the classroom in order to avoid becoming distracted during lectures.
Reflective Learners	• Learn by thinking about the information—pondering it • Say, "Let me think about this for a while." • Enjoy working alone • Learn best by carefully considering the information that is presented to them • Are typically intrapersonal, logical, mathematical learners • Tend to be "thinker" personality types	• Stop to review what you've read and think of possible questions while reading. • Write short summaries of readings in your own words. • Study in quiet environments free from distractions. • Avoid memorizing subject matter. • Answer questions: who, where, what, when, why, how? • Summarize subject matter and apply it to your world.
Sensing Learners	• Like to learn facts • Don't like surprises • Like to learn things by established methods • Are good with details • Are good at memorization • Enjoy hands-on (like lab) work • Tend to be practical and careful when learning	• Ask your professor for examples of concepts and procedures in class. • Try to find specific examples of concepts in your course textbook or other references. • Brainstorm with friends or classmates about the details of a topic.
Intuitive Learners	• Like to independently discover ideas • Dislike repetition • Like innovation and surprise • Are good at grasping new concepts • Are good with abstract ideas • Learn quickly and are innovative	• Be aware that you may be bored in a class that uses detailed materials that need to be memorized. • Ask the instructor for interpretations or theories that link these materials together. • Read the entire question before you start answering when taking tests, and be sure to check your answers before submitting the exam.
Verbal Learners	• Do better with words (i.e., verbal—spoken or discussed—directions or information) and audio books • Are frequently talkative in class • Prefer presenting oral reports rather than written reports • Enjoy debates and discussions • Benefit from reading aloud • Tend to memorize well, including names • Prefer listening to the news • May need verbal explanation of maps, diagrams, or graphs • Enjoy speaking with others • Enjoy music and sing frequently • Are often good at foreign languages • Must repeat information such as phone numbers • Benefit from study groups • Read slowly • Tend to be articulate speakers	• Write the outline of your course material and transcribe notes from class in your own words. • Work with another person who is in the class and explain material to each other verbally. • Utilize audiotapes for learning. • Read information, including steps to take, aloud when studying. • Ask questions. • Use word association techniques to remember facts. • Participate in class discussions. • Record directions and notes. • Avoid auditory distractions. • Participate in a study group or study with a study partner. • Make up songs or rhymes to go along with the pertinent material. • Use rhymes to recall dates, names, facts, etc.

(continues)

Table 6.1 Learning Style Descriptions and Tips for Studying* *(continued)*

Learning Style Preference	Description of Learners	Tips for Studying
Visual Learners	• Relate best to information that is written, such as graphs, maps, diagrams, charts, highlighted notes, flashcards, etc. • Describe things they see in terms of appearances • Love magazines, books, and other types of reading material • Must have a quiet place to study • Benefit from making their own notes, even from information already printed, and may feel frustrated when unable to do so • Have difficulty following lectures that are long • Prefer often to sit toward the front of the class • Are often good writers, scoring high on written assignments • May demonstrate outstanding photographic memory • Can remember precisely where information is located on a page • Tend to be good at spelling • Tend to be detail oriented • Are typically tidy and organized • Ask often for verbal directions to be repeated	• Try to find visual materials that represent course material. • Ask your instructor if there are any videotapes or DVDs of course material. • Develop a map of the concepts that you are learning—including boxes, circles, lines, arrows, and flow charts between concepts to show connections. • Write down key points or color-code key points in a chapter or in your notes with a highlighter so that things related to one topic are the same color. • Ask for written directions. • Visualize spelling of words or facts that must be memorized. • Copy what is on the board. • Sit near the front of the classroom. • Utilize illustrations to remember important material. • Utilize visual metaphors to associate relevant content. • Write down explanations for points that are difficult.
Global Learners	• Might have trouble with content details until the "bigger picture" is understood • Might still be unclear about the details even when they get the big picture • Tend to learn material in large jumps—taking in material almost randomly without seeing connections—and then suddenly "getting it" • Might be able to solve complex problems quickly or to put ideas together in new ways after they have grasped the big picture—but they might find it hard to explain how they did this	• Skim through a chapter in the textbook to get the overall view—since the big picture is needed to understand material—before beginning to study details. • Try to immerse yourself in individual topics for larger blocks of time instead of studying for a short time on different subjects each night. • Try to relate the subject to things you already know. • Pay attention to outlines. Outlines will help you establish a framework for "storing" new information • Don't skip the introduction or summary. You will benefit from reading these before you read the actual book. • Look for boundaries. Global learners may have trouble discerning where one concept or event ends and another begins. It might be helpful for you to establish concrete beginning and ending points. • Ask for examples. Your brain likes to make comparisons, so the more examples, the better. Write down the examples, but label them as examples so you're not confused later. • Draw timelines. This is another way of creating boundaries. Your brain likes them.
Sequential Learners	• Might not completely understand the entire topic, but can do something with it (like pass a test or solve a problem) • Know a lot about specific parts of the subject but might have trouble relating the individual parts to the larger subject or to different subjects • May feel the need to understand each part of an algebra equation • Might be good with time management and are usually punctual • Tend to remember names • Tend to divide and label notes to categorize things • Tend to plan ahead • Tend to respond to problems with logic first instead of emotions	• Ask the instructor to fill in the skipped steps if he or she jumps from topic to topic. • Take time to make an outline of the course concepts in logical order when you study. • Ask for clear rules; without them you feel lost. • Don't worry about not finishing something; you might not want to move on to a new task if something interferes with your work. Try not to get hung up but move on and re-visit the project later. • Group your information into categories. • Sit at the front of class to avoid distractions. • Ask for the specific goals of a project; you might need to understand the goals before you can get into the project.

*Table adapted from: Felder, R. M. and Soloman, B. A. *Learning Styles and Strategies.* A four-page handout briefly explaining the learning style preferences obtained using the *Index of Learning Styles*. Used with permission, and available at: **http://bvtlab.com/B6J99**

_________. *Understanding Your Learning Styles*. Available at: http://bvtlab.com/5Gg5g; Copyright 2008
Website: http://www.pssc.ttu.edu/techhort/lasrvy/a_r.htm (http://bvtlab.com/6Qb76)
Website: http://homeworktips.about.com/od/homeworkhelp/a/global.htm (http://bvtlab.com/74K5f)

Additional information about learning styles and the Felder-Silverman model may be found at the *Index of Learning Styles (ILS)* webpage: (**http://bvtlab.com/56c3w**). Much of the information in this chapter has been adapted from resources on that webpage.

6.4 Practice What You Have Learned

Now that you have read about various learning styles and how they compare to each other, you should complete the Assignment 6.1 Learning Styles Application Report. Step-by-step instructions for the assignment are given at the end of this chapter. As a part of the assignment, you will complete your own *ILS*.

In order to help you understand how to interpret your own *ILS*, let's look at the example provided in Figure 6.2. The scores for the example student are indicated by an "X" over the number.

Figure 6.2 ***Index of Learning Style*** **Results (NC State University)**

Index of Learning Styles (ILS) Results

Results for: Example Student

ACT									X				REF
	11	9	7	5	3	1	1	3	5	7	9	11	
SEN												X	INT
	11	9	7	5	3	1	1	3	5	7	9	11	
VIS				X									VRB
	11	9	7	5	3	1	1	3	5	7	9	11	
SEQ										X			GLO
	11	9	7	5	3	1	1	3	5	7	9	11	

- If your score on a scale is 1-3, you are fairly well balanced on the two dimensions of that scale.
- If your score on a scale is 5-7, you have a moderate preference for one dimension of the scale and will learn more easily in a teaching environment which favors that dimension.
- If your score on a scale is 9-11, you have a very strong preference for one dimension of the scale. You may have real difficulty learning in an environment that does not support that preference.

Analyzing Your *ILS* Results

Let's look at the results for the "Example Student" in Figure 6.2. How would he or she interpret the results? What learning styles does the student prefer? Well, if we look at the first scale, "ACT" versus "REF," we see that the scale goes from 1 in the center to 11 at each of the end-points, "Active" and "Reflective." The student scored a 5 on the reflective side of this scale, which translates to a moderate preference for reflective learning. This means that such a student typically learns more easily in a teaching environment that favors reflective learning.

Following that example, we can see that the student scored an 11 on the "INT" side of "SEN" versus "INT" (Sensing … Intuitive), meaning he or she has a very strong preference for intuitive learning compared to sensory learning. Because the preference is so strong here, the student might have real problems learning in an environment that doesn't support intuitive learning. (Hmm … Maybe this helps explain my own difficulty in learning chemistry?) Remember that sensing learners tend to focus on sights and physical sensations—and that they tend to be concrete, practical, methodical, and oriented toward facts and hands-on procedures.[5] Intuitive learners learn better in courses that are abstract and include theories and models. (In fact, I do love—and learn much more easily in—courses that deal with theory and thinking compared to hands-on lab courses.)

The sample student scored a 5 on the visual end of the "VIS" versus "VRB" (Visual … Verbal) scale. He or she has a moderate preference for visual learning and would learn better when looking at charts, graphs, pictures, and diagrams—and not so well with spoken explanations.

On the "SEQ" (Sequential) versus "GLO" (Global) scale, the example student's score of 7 on the "GLO" end would indicate a moderate preference for global learning. He or she would tend to learn better when learning in a systems-oriented manner and would tend to look at the big picture before settling down to understanding the details of a situation or topic.

In case, my *ILS* results do mirror my own understanding of how I learn. I always thought I was a more reflective, intuitive, visual, and global learner. Throughout my education, I've had trouble with courses and material that were fact-based, with lots of details (like chemistry) and lots of memorization. Courses in which the instructor lectures 100 percent of the time have also been difficult for me. When I had courses like that, I took notes and made charts to help myself understand materials. But if you think you are a sensory learner, and the *ILS* scores you as a 9 on the "INT" scale, not to worry. Don't discount your own judgment of your learning preferences—that is, trust your gut over the test. You may want to consider re-taking the test, as well, to see if your scores change at a later date (because learning preferences can change over time).

There are a couple of things to remember here, too. One is that your learning style preferences are dependent on the situation, and you can switch from one to the other depending on what your learning environment is like. You don't always use just one type of learning style; instead, you shift between them to a greater or lesser degree, depending on your own flexibility in learning. The ability to shift your learning style to match the style in which the new information is presented is a mark of intelligence and is something that you want to work on throughout your college career. You'll be more successful if you can switch between learning styles in order to match each professor's teaching style.

Second, remember that learning style preferences are not written in stone—and should never be used to determine whether or not you can accomplish something. Even if you are not sensory, visual, or active in your learning, for example, you can still be an engineer, scientist, or nurse. And unfortunately, if your preferred learning style does not match the professor's teaching style (or the subject matter's particular presentation), that still does not excuse getting a D on the exam!

Want to learn more?

Try these resources.

For more information about the learning styles model and implications of learning styles for instructors and students, visit:
http://bvtlab.com/Fr6mM

Richard Felder's Home Page:
http://bvtlab.com/6ANs3

Various websites about learning and learning styles:
http://bvtlab.com/A8JDZ

The *Index of Learning Styles* is a self-scoring questionnaire for assessing preferences on four dimensions of the Felder-Silverman model.
http://bvtlab.com/66467

Descriptions of Learning Styles: A four-page handout that briefly explains the learning style preferences obtained using the *Index of Learning Styles*.
http://bvtlab.com/6q6a9

The *Index of Learning Styles (ILS)* is not meant for use as a guide for curriculum change or determining career choices, and it would not be an appropriate use of the tool to do so.[5] Instead, it is meant as a guide to understanding how *you* learn best—or within which types of learning environments do you learn more easily and which are more difficult for you. Knowing your own personal learning preferences helps you to understand when and where you might need to do extra work or spend extra time in order to take in and understand new materials. Use the *ILS* throughout your college career to check in with your own understanding of how you learn best; your results will probably change as you grow intellectually and conceptually.

Reading Comprehension Question 6.4 (Analysis)

What is the main purpose for this chapter on learning styles?

a. To provide the student with a way to change their learning style
b. To make the student aware of their individual learning style so they can use it for maximum success
c. To make the professor use specific techniques to help students learn in a deeper way
d. To provide the student with information about college classes

SUMMARY

In this chapter you learned about different learning styles, as well as strategies for being successful with different learning styles. In addition, you took a test (the *Index of Learning Styles*) to determine your own individual learning style preferences and interpreted the results. You also thought about some strategies for being successful in your coursework. The more you know about your own learning styles and how to adapt in various situations, the more successful you will be in college. It may be interesting for you to keep track of your learning style, study strategies, and intellectual development as you go through college to see how much you are changing and growing.

REVIEW QUESTIONS 6.1

Instructions: Following are five true-false statements taken from the information in this chapter. First, try to answer them without looking back at the chapter. Then review the chapter to see how well you did.

Question & Answer	Rationale
Circle true or false for each of the following statements.	**Write an explanation stating why each statement is true or false.**
1. An individual's orientation to learning can be summed up by two components: learning style preferences and chronological age. **True or False**	Your Rationale:
2. Knowing your own personal learning preferences helps you to understand when and where you might need to do extra work or spend extra time in order to take in and to understand new materials. **True or False**	Your Rationale:
3. The more you know about your own learning styles and how to adapt in various situations, the more successful you will be in college. **True or False**	Your Rationale:
4. The *ILS* measures a person's learning style and can tell you for which profession you are best suited. **True or False**	Your Rationale:
5. Everybody with active and sensing learning preferences makes better grades than those who are reflective, intuitive learners. **True or False**	Your Rationale:

Name: ______________________________

Chapter Six

Study Guide

Chapter 6, Goal 1: The student will be able to describe eight types of learners and learning styles.

Questions	Answers & Notes

Name: ____________________

Chapter Six

Study Guide

Chapter 6, Goal 2: The student will be able to analyze his or her own personal learning preferences using the *Index of Learning Styles (ILS)*.

Questions	Answers & Notes

Name: ______________________________

Chapter Six **Study Guide**

Chapter 6, Goal 3: The student will be able to list at least two study strategies that will help him or her learn more effectively based on his or her learning styles.

Questions	Answers & Notes

Name: ________________________________

Preparing for Class:
Use This Page to Record Questions or Insights to Discuss in Class.

Assignment 6.1

Learning Style Assessment

Instructions: This assessment will help you to figure out which learning styles work best for you. Then you can use the information in this chapter to plan some study strategies that will improve the effectiveness of your studying.

Step 1: Complete the *Index of Learning Styles (ILS)* survey at the following website: **http://bvtlab.com/8W873**

After you finish the survey, the website will show you your results. They will look similar to the ones depicted in Figure 6.2.

Step 2: Print your results and save them.

Step 3: Look at your results' page to determine which learning styles best fit you. Use your results to answer the questions on the form on the following page.

The results' page presents a number line with a code for a different learning style preference on each end. For example, "ACT" is the code for the active learning style and "REF" is the code for the reflective learning style. There will be an X over one of the numbers on the number line. The X will be closer to one of the learning style codes than it is to the other. It will be closer to the style that you are most comfortable using based on the answers you gave for the *ILS* survey questions. The number score indicates how strongly you prefer that particular style compared to the style on the opposite side of the number line.

We can use Figure 6.2 in Chapter 6 as an example. In the example, the X is placed over the number 5 that is closer to "REF" (Reflective). This means that the person who completed the survey has a stronger preference for the reflective learning style ("REF") than for the active learning style ("ACT"). Since the score is 5, we infer that this person has a moderate preference for the reflective style of learning. A lower score (such as 1 or 3) would suggest a mild preference. A score of 5–7 would indicate a moderate level of preferences, and a score of 9–11 would indicate a strong preference.

Step 4: A very important question on the form is "Given your preferences, what are some **specific study strategies** that you can use?" Review the information in this chapter, and think of some specific study strategies that you could use that match your particular learning styles. Write these strategies down, and consider adding them to your study regimen. You may need to add some of these strategies to your study session tickets (the ones you created after reading Chapter 2).

NOTES

ASSIGNMENT 6.1

Index of Learning Styles: My Results and Analysis

1. Are you more of an active learner or a reflective learner?

   A. Based on your results' page, which learning style do you prefer: active ("ACT") or reflective ("REF")?
   ____

   B. What was your numeric score? ___________

   C. Based on your score how strongly do you prefer this particular learning style? ___________

   D. Given that you are more (circle one → active / reflective), what are some specific study strategies that you could use? (List below)

2. Are you more of a sensory learner or an intuitive learner?

   A. Based on your results' page, which learning style do you prefer: sensory ("SEN") or intuitive ("INT")?
   ____

   B. What was your numeric score? ___________

   C. Based on your score how strongly do you prefer this particular learning style? ___________

   D. Given that you are more (circle one → sensory / intuitive), what are some specific study strategies that you could use? (List below)

NOTES

Assignment 6.1

Index of Learning Styles: My Results and Analysis (*continued*)

3. Are you more of a visual learner or a verbal learner?

   A. Based on your results' page, which learning style do you prefer: visual ("VIS") or verbal ("VER")?
   ____

   B. What was your numeric score? ____________

   C. Based on your score how strongly do you prefer this particular learning style? ____________

   D. Given that you are more (circle one → visual / verbal), what are some specific study strategies that you could use? (List below)

4. Are you more of a sequential learner or a global learner?

   A. Based on your results' page, which learning style do you prefer: sequential ("SEQ") or global ("GLO")? ____________________

   B. What was your numeric score? ____________

   C. Based on your score how strongly do you prefer this particular learning style? ____________

   D. Given that you are more (circle one → sequential / global), what are some specific study strategies that you could use? (List below)

Chapter 7 Roadmap

Writing College Papers: I Have a Paper Due!

In this chapter you will examine some guidelines for writing a formal, college-level paper. You will also learn how to plan and organize your writing efforts for maximum success.

This chapter roadmap page presents the formal learning goals for this chapter and a checklist that you should follow as you read and study the chapter.

Student Learning Goals for This Chapter

After completing this chapter the student should be able to do the following:

1. Identify and apply guidelines for writing a college-level paper.
2. Distinguish between peer-reviewed journal articles and other types of literature.
3. Apply specified style manual rules (such as MLA or APA) to a college-level paper.
4. Apply basic formatting tips when writing either a general college-level paper or a research paper.
5. Understand the process (steps) for creating a formal college-level paper.
6. Design a plan for creating a research paper over a reasonable span of time.

Checklist for This Chapter

Target date/ deadline	Check when completed	Activity
________	❑	1. Complete Critical Thinking Activity 7.1.
________	❑	2. Convert the learning goals above to questions that you can answer as you read the chapter. Write your questions on the study guide pages near the end of this chapter.
________	❑	3. Read the chapter.
________	❑	4. Try to answer the reading comprehension questions as you come to them in the chapter. Check each answer by comparing it to the list of correct answers in the back of the book. If any answer was not correct, then review the passages preceding the question to see why you missed the question.
________	❑	5. Use the study guide pages near the end of this chapter to answer the questions you created in Step 2. Once completed, these pages will be your study guide.
________	❑	6. Write down any questions, insights, or comments that you have as you read so that you can bring them up in class (if applicable).
________	❑	7. Complete Review Questions 7.1.
________	❑	8. Complete Assignment 7.1.

CRITICAL THINKING ACTIVITY 7.1

As a way to begin thinking about the topic of this chapter, please consider the following questions and write your answers in the space provided.

Do you think you could eat a whole pizza by yourself?

Your answer is likely, "Sure I can," because you know that pizzas come in many sizes including a small, individual serving size.

Imagine, however, a pizza that is six feet in diameter—a pizza that, if you stood it up in one end, would be taller than most people.

Here is your assignment:

Design a plan that would enable you to eat—all by yourself—an entire pizza that is six feet in diameter. Record the steps of your plan in the space provided below on this page. Be prepared to share your plan in class (if applicable).

Writing College Papers:
I Have a Paper Due!

7

When asked, 'How do you write?' I invariably answer, 'One word at a time,' and the answer is invariably dismissed. But that is all it is. It sounds too simple to be true, but consider the Great Wall of China, if you will: one stone at a time, man. That's all. One stone at a time.

— *Stephen King*[1]

The most important thing is to read as much as you can, like I did. It will give you an understanding of what makes good writing and it will enlarge your vocabulary.

— *J. K. Rowling*[2]

As a college student, you will be asked to do many types of writing. The following four basic categories of writing assignments are typically used in college: personal writing, academic writing, public writing, and creative writing. Personal writing, when used as an assignment, includes things like personal journal responses, in-class essay responses, and shorter opinion paper assignments. Academic writing includes research papers, analysis papers, article reviews or summaries, more formal in-class essays, and essay exams. The purpose of academic writing is to allow the student to demonstrate understanding. Public writing is identified as writing for an outside audience and includes resumes, business letters, and so on. Creative writing, or writing for creative expression, includes poetry and short stories.

In this chapter you will learn some basic tips for writing that will apply to any writing assignment, and you will learn some more specific guidelines that apply to writing a research paper. You will also learn how to plan for writing a research paper or similar writing project, because those types of writing assignments cannot be completed in a single sitting. You will need to plan when you will complete each step in the process of writing a research paper.

7.1 Guidelines for College Writing

It may be helpful to review these tips before beginning a formal writing assignment.

1. Follow the professor's instructions

Different professors may require different formats or other particulars for the paper. Even within the same course, different writing assignments may have different requirements. For example, a research paper has different content and format restrictions than an opinion essay. Make sure to find out what the specific requirements are for each writing assignment, and then make sure that you follow those instructions.

Sometimes students do silly things with the formatting of a written assignment—such as using a very large font or very large margins to make the paper appear longer. Your professor is not an idiot. He or she will recognize this manipulation immediately. The professor will not be impressed; instead, it sets low expectations for your paper.

2. Use the proper format

How will you format your paper? There are many different styles that are used in college and professional research publications. Four commonly used style guides are the American Psychological Association (APA), the Modern Language Association (MLA), the Chicago Manual of Style (CMS), and the Council of Science Editors (CSE). APA is the style most commonly used within the social and behavioral sciences. MLA is the style most commonly used within the liberal arts and humanities. CMS is the style often used by researchers of history. CSE is often used within science disciplines. These four are not the only styles that are used, but they are the ones that you are most likely to encounter during your undergraduate education.

If your professor requires a particular style guide (such as MLA or APA) for the writing assignment, take the time to look at the guide and make sure that your paper conforms to the proper format. Most of the style guides are available in the library, and college library websites often have links to information about the various formats. Make sure that you are using the most current version of the guide or the version that your professor has specified.

Online Resources for Style Guides

Research and Documentation Online is a website version of the book, *Research and Documentation in the Electronic Age,* 5th Edition, by Diana Hacker and Barbara Fister. This website provides information about MLA, APA, CMS, and CSE—including example papers. Following is the URL for this website:

http://bvtlab.com/89286

The *Perdue Online Writing Lab* (OWL) has many excellent resources for information about the different style guides. A very useful resource is the "Comparison Chart for MLA, APA, and CMS." It is a table that shows examples side-by-side from each of the three styles for the most common formatting questions. You can download it as a PDF file from the following URL:

http://bvtlab.com/98w2S

The APA website offers a very impressive online tutorial complete with downloadable examples where you can learn almost anything you need to know about formatting in APA style. You can access the *Basics of APA Style Tutorial* online at the following URL:

http://bvtlab.com/6866R

The Chicago Manual of Style Online is a website where information about the CMS and updates for the CMS are posted. You can access it at the following URL:

http://bvtlab.com/mu9Z7

3. Do not plagiarize, and keep a copy of your sources

When you use the actual words or even just the ideas of others in a paper, you must give credit to the original author. This is usually done by including a citation for the quote or idea within the paper and a reference identifying the original source at the end of the paper. Failure to properly cite the use of another's ideas is called plagiarism. The penalty for plagiarism can be very severe. Ask the professor if you are unsure about some part of your paper. Check and correct before you submit the paper.

It is very important that you avoid plagiarism when you write a research paper. Sometimes students are inadvertently guilty of plagiarism. However, it does not matter whether or not the student did it intentionally when the professor sits down to grade the essay. The professor has no choice but to assign a grade of zero to a plagiarized paper because he or she may not be able, by reading, to determine your intent. It is the student's solemn responsibility to avoid plagiarism.

Copying from a book (or other source) without properly identifying the source is plagiarism. It is particularly problematic for a graded assignment because copying does not demonstrate understanding. A first grader could copy from the book, but would be unlikely to understand what he or she has written. What you write in your research paper should demonstrate that you understand the concept about which you are writing.

It is important that you understand what plagiarism is and that you take care to do your own thinking and to write in such a way so as to demonstrate your understanding of the topic. The process of thinking about the topic and putting it into your own words, possibly with your own examples, will help you own the information and forge it into your long-term memory.

Quoting from the textbook or other sources is permissible when it is properly cited, but it is not acceptable to submit an essay that is basically just one big quote. Try to convey your thoughts with a combination of quotes and paraphrased concepts in your own words. In many cases, using your own examples of the concept (instead of copying examples from the textbook) is a good way to demonstrate understanding. It is also acceptable to challenge or question ideas presented in a book or an article.

The easiest way to avoid plagiarism is to include citations in your essay so that the original author is credited for their words or ideas. Citations in a paper may impress the professor during grading because the citations suggest that the student has read and thought about the articles or other resources that were cited. Such a paper may be more impressive than one in which the student presents nothing but his or her own opinion—without any evidence of prior reading or study. However, the citations in your paper must conform to a specified format. There are many different styles or formats for citations, so remember to ask your professor what style is required for each assignment.

Keep copies of the articles you use in your paper until after the paper has been graded, because the professor may ask to see some of them. If the topic of your paper is one that you are likely to study again in another course, then you may wish to keep those copies of your sources for future reference. You will not be allowed to submit the same exact paper again, but you may write a new paper on a similar topic for which some of the same references will be useful.

4. Write with purpose

Make sure that the paper demonstrates your mastery of the topic or assignment. Provide support for the main points in the paper with details—such as examples, explanations, and references to supporting documents (with citations).

Following are a few general tips for writing any type of paper and also a few tips to use when writing a research paper. Follow these guidelines unless your professor tells you to do something differently.

Tips for general writing

- Create an outline and use it to write your paper. It may be helpful to write your first draft on top of your outline—filling in the text under each section of the outline. Even if you delete the outline from the paper after you have finished it, an outline is a good tool to help you organize your thinking during the writing process.

- Use introductory sentences. Don't just launch into a main section of your paper without informing the reader of the "big picture."

- Use transitional sentences. These are sentences that bridge the different parts of your paper, connecting them together. Include them at the end of one main part of your paper to prepare the reader for the next main section of your paper.

- Do not quote the dictionary in your paper. As McEnerney and Williams from the University of Chicago Writing Program have explained, "If a concept is so important to your paper that you feel compelled to specify its meaning, its dictionary definition will be too generic for your purposes. A somewhat better strategy here is to cite a definition by a specialist in a particular field or by an otherwise admirable individual."[3]

- Avoid redundancy.

Tips for writing a research paper

- Do not put your personal opinion or anecdotal stories in the paper because these are not appropriate for a formal research paper. A research paper presents the findings and analysis of research projects that were conducted on the topic you are writing about. You can use your own words to summarize the research, but do not include your own unverified opinion.
- Do not use Wikipedia as a source for a research paper, because Wikipedia articles are not original research and are not refereed—so they may not be accurate. However, you may read Wikipedia articles to get ideas about a topic and then look up the original research Wikipedia cites.
- Use current sources that are no more than about five years old. Including an older, famous foundational article or including a series of articles that go far back in history to establish a historical perspective would be exceptions to this rule. Ask your professor to be sure with regard to any specific assignment, but it is generally expected that the sources for a research paper be very current. (This may be more true for the sciences than other fields; even English majors write research papers, but their field changes more slowly, the age or the source isn't relevant.)
- Use primary research and refereed journal articles describing original research. You should not use opinion pieces or articles that summarize research conducted by someone other than the author. Instead, get the original article written by the author who actually conducted the research.
- Remember that personal pronouns (such as *I*, *we*, and *you*), contractions (such as *don't* and *can't*), and colloquial language or slang are almost always inappropriate for this kind of assignment.
- Consult the appropriate style guide for formatting rules—including when to use numerals and when to write out numbers.
- Do not use vague terms to describe the findings of research (for example, "A good many of the respondents agreed ..."). Instead, be specific and accurate (for example, "Fifty percent of the respondents agreed ...").
- Be aware that the term *significant* has a special mathematical meaning in research. Therefore, you should not use the word *significant* unless you are reporting on a test of significance that was performed. In cases where a measure of significance was used, do not describe it in terms of varying degree (for example, it was "a little" or "somewhat" or "the most" significant). There are no degrees of significance; instead you would report that the results either were or were not significant.

5. Proofread, do your best work, and grade yourself first

The paper you submit for a grade should be a polished product. It should reflect your best effort. Therefore, never submit your first draft. Instead, review your paper, and make corrections or improvements. This is called proofreading. It is kind of like grading yourself. Don't let the professor become your proofreader. You need to find the problems and fix them first so that the professor never sees them.

Make sure that your paper has correct spelling, grammatical construction, and punctuation before you submit it. Your essay must also be written in complete sentences. It must make sense. As part of the proofreading process, you should read the paper **aloud** to yourself to check for clarity. It is also advisable that you ask a friend or a tutor to look over your paper. A fresh pair of eyes may quickly see errors that you have overlooked. This way you can do one final edit and correct those errors before you submit your paper for a grade.

Reading Comprehension Question 7.1 (Knowledge)

Susan has written a paper on adolescent pregnancy and has copied two paragraphs from a journal article. She has not given a citation for the paragraphs that she used. This would be which of the following?

a. This would be okay, if she types the paragraphs verbatim.

b. This would be a problem if the paragraphs do not support her thesis.

c. This would be plagiarism, for which there may be severe penalties.

d. This would be a way for Susan to show her professor how much she knows.

7.2 Resources for College Writing

In most cases, when you have a formal college writing assignment, you will need to find resources to inform and support your writing. Usually, the best place to find those resources is the college library and its website.

1. Using sources from the Internet

The Internet can be a great resource for your writing, but you must take care how you use it. Unlike refereed journals, much of the information on the Internet is not reviewed or validated in any way. If you are not careful, you could wind up putting inaccurate information in your paper because you got the information from an unreliable source. As the website for UC Berkeley explains,

> The burden is on you—the reader—to establish the validity, authorship, timeliness, and integrity of what you find. Documents can easily be copied and falsified or copied with omissions and errors—intentional or accidental. In the general World Wide Web, there are no editors (unlike most print publications) to proofread and "send it back" or "reject it" until it meets the standards of a publishing house's reputation. Most pages found in general search engines for the web are self-published or published by businesses, both small and large, with motives to get you to buy something or believe a point of view. Even within university and library web sites, there can be many pages that the institution does not try to oversee. The web **needs** to be free like that. If you want to use it for serious research, **you** need to cultivate the habit of healthy skepticism, of questioning everything you find with critical thinking.[4]

2. Using scholarly publications

As already mentioned, unlike the Internet, refereed scholarly journal articles are a reliable source for information. This is especially important when you are writing a research paper.

What is a scholarly journal? Generally, scholarly journals have a sober, serious look. They often contain many graphs and charts with few glossy pages or exciting pictures. In addition, scholarly journals always cite their sources in the form of footnotes or bibliographies. Articles are written by a scholar in the field or by someone who has done research in the field. Furthermore, the language of scholarly journals is that of the discipline covered, and they assume some scholarly background on the part of the reader. The main purpose of a scholarly journal is to report on original research or experimentation in order to make such information available to the rest of the scholarly world. Many scholarly journals—though by no means all—are published by a specific professional organization.

The articles that you will find in a scholarly journal almost always follow the same basic outline. They start with an abstract and end with a list of references. Following are the headings that you almost always see in a research journal article:

Title	The title and author(s) name(s) appear at the top, often with information about the author's affiliation(s).
Abstract	This summary helps the reader to determine how relevant this study is to the reader's interests.
Literature review	This is where the author(s) briefly describes previous research on the topic and shows where the current study fits into an overall understanding of the topic.
Purpose of the study	This section often includes the hypothesis and problem statement.
Methodology	This section describes the research design and procedures.
Findings	This section describes the results obtained by the methods previously described. Here is where you see if the hypothesis was supported or not. It presents data only and does not include opinion.
Discussion	This section is where the author(s) discusses what he or she thinks the findings mean.
Conclusion	This section serves as a summary and often discusses implications or ideas for future studies.
References	This section is where you will find the works cited in a research article.

In addition, you will see that tables, charts, figures, and statistical data are often found throughout the article. A few examples of scholarly journals include the following:

- *American Economic Review*
- *Archives of Sexual Behavior*
- *JAMA: The Journal of the American Medical Association*
- *Journal of Marriage and the Family*
- *Modern Fiction Studies*
- *Sex Roles: A Journal of Research*

Examples of publications that are not considered scholarly include newspapers (such as the *Atlanta Journal*), popular magazines (such as *Newsweek*), and journals of opinion (such as *The New Republic*).

If you are looking for scholarly journals, then you should connect to the webpage for the college library. That is your best source for scholarly articles; and best of all—it is free.

Reading Comprehension Question 7.2 (Literal Comprehension)

Which of the following is true about writing a research paper for college?

a. It is usually easy to decide on a topic for a research paper

b. Searching for materials to support your research topic is a quick and easy task

c. A paper should be researched, written, edited, and rewritten before it is submitted to the professor.

d. None of the above

Want to learn more?

Try these resources.

The Purdue Online Writing Lab offers information and tips on different types of writing.
http://bvtlab.com/P7R97

An excellent resource for students learning to write college-level papers is the book, *Writing in College: A Short Guide to College Writing* by Joseph M. Williams and Lawrence McEnerney. This resource is available at the following URL for the University of Chicago website and is part of the University of Chicago Writing Program:
http://bvtlab.com/cC273

Another outstanding resource, found at the following URL, is the article, "What is an academic paper?" written by Karen Gocsik of Dartmouth College. It is part of the Dartmouth Writing Program:
http://bvtlab.com/7FF62

Reading Comprehension Question 7.3 (Inferential Comprehension)

You have chosen to do a research paper on techniques for success in college. Which of the following is most likely to be scholarly and refereed?

a. An article on a website selling books and DVDs on how to make straight A's
b. An article in the *Atlanta Journal Constitution* newspaper
c. An article you found in the library, in a journal, that includes an abstract, a literature review section, a methods section, a findings section, and a references list
d. An article from Wikipedia

7.3 Planning the College-Level Paper

Writing a formal paper in college usually involves several steps: (1) selecting a topic, (2) collecting information about the topic, (3) reading and thinking about the information, (4) writing the first draft, (5) proofreading, and (6) producing the final copy. If the formal paper is a research paper or if it involves a project or experiment, then additional steps may be required. It should be clear, then, that most formal college-level writing cannot be done in a single day. It is a task that you will have to divide into smaller parts, or steps, which you will complete over time.

Consider the critical thinking exercise that appears at the beginning of this chapter. On that page, you were asked to devise a plan whereby you could eat a pizza of six feet in diameter all by yourself. At first you might muse that such a task is impossible because it is far too much for any human to eat in one sitting. However, almost anyone could eat the giant pizza if they simply broke it up into many smaller meals and ate them one at a time over many days.

Writing a formal college-level paper is like eating a giant pizza, in that it is not something that you can complete in one sitting on one day. It is nearly impossible for you to do your best work on a paper if you try to write the entire paper in one day or one weekend. You need to **break the large task of writing the paper into the smaller tasks** (or steps) that are involved in writing the paper. Then simply plan a time to complete each smaller task so that everything is complete before the deadline. You can **use the calendars** and **task list templates** provided in this book to plan your college writing project.

So, how do you plan a major college writing project? First, you should estimate how much time each step will require. Second, working backward from the due date, mark each step on your calendar, adding each step to the task list for those dates.

1. Identify the tasks involved and estimate the time required for each

In the example depicted below (see Tables 7.1 and 7.2), you can see how a student might plan the date on which to begin a writing project and the various dates on which to complete each step. Please note that the estimates listed in this example may not accurately reflect the amounts of time that you will need for a similar project. It is also true that your personal task list may vary from the items in this example. The estimates for each actual assignment will vary based on the requirements for the assignment and how long it takes you to read your sources and write your draft. Therefore, you will have to make your own time estimates for your writing project. Try to make your estimates as realistic as you can. After you have more experience with writing college papers, you will be better at accurately predicting the time required for various tasks.

Reading Comprehension Question 7.4 (Analysis)

The main idea of the passage above, entitled "Planning the College-Level Paper," is which of the following?

a. Planning a paper ahead of time is not necessary in college.

b. Planning the paper can help you to write and revise the paper in time to turn it in.

c. Planning a project takes time that most students do not have in college.

d. Planning a paper ahead of time is not an efficient use of a student's time.

Table 7.1 Task List Planning Example

Step	Time Estimate
1. Select a topic.	
A. Look at a few resources in the library and/or online to make sure that enough information on the topic is easily available.	1 hour
B. Get the topic approved by the professor (after class or during the professor's office hours).	5 to 10 minutes
2. Collect information about the topic.	
A. Search for sources in the library and/or online.	2 hours
B. Think about how the sources could be put together to support a topic and about how the topic may be narrowed.	1 hour
C. Read initial sources and make notes.	2 hours
3. Study (think more deeply about) the information that you collected on the topic.	
A. Identify questions about, or aspects of, your topic that were not adequately covered by the initial sources.	30 minutes
B. Survey the initial sources for leads to additional sources.	30 minutes
C. Collect additional sources.	2 hours
D. Read additional sources and make notes.	2 hours
4. Write the first draft.	
A. Create an outline.	30 minutes
B. Write the text that fills in the various sections of the outline, citing sources as appropriate.	2 hours
C. Continue writing the text.	2 hours
D. Create the reference list.	1 hour
E. Write the introduction/abstract.	30 minutes
5. Proofread and revise	
A. Read the paper aloud to make sure that it makes sense.	1 hour
B. Check for grammar and spelling errors.	30 minutes
C. Check each citation to make sure that it matches the reference list.	30 minutes
D. Check the entire paper for format compliance to whichever style guide the professor requires.	30 minutes
E. Make corrections to errors found in the steps above.	1 hour
F. Proofread aloud, a second time, to make sure that all of the errors were corrected.	1 hour
G. Print the final copy and prepare it for submission.	30 minutes
6. Submit	

2. Add the tasks to calendar

Once you have identified the tasks associated with writing the paper and estimated the amount of time each item will require, you should record the tasks as appointments on your monthly calendar and on the task list (to-do checklist) for each day affected.

Even though the total amount of time required to complete the project is less than 24 hours (if the time estimates on the task list planning example are accurate), it cannot be done in only one or two days. These tasks have to be done over a period of time with some time to think between tasks. (You may have noticed by now that you are supposed to do a lot of thinking in college.)

Following (Table 7.2) is an example of a monthly calendar with times allocated to complete each individual project task, or step. To figure out when you should do each step, simply start with the last one (Task #6 Submitting the paper on the due date), and work your way backward through the calendar. Schedule the steps at times that fit within your regular schedule and in reverse order (5, 4, 3, 2, and finally 1). Note that in this example, the student has left a two-day gap between when the **final paper is printed** and the **actual due date**. This gap was planned so that the student would be prepared to deal with any last-minute delays that might arise, such as a broken printer or the discovery that more time is needed to correct errors than was expected. Do not wait until the due date to complete assignments. Plan ahead so that you can do your best work. Once again, as with many other academic endeavors, good planning is a key to success in college-level writing.

Table 7.2 Example Monthly Calendar with Tasks Planned

Mon	Tue	Wed	Thu	Fri	Sat	Sun
1 Step 1A START DATE	2 Step 1B	3	4 Step 2A	5	6	7
8 Step 2B	9 Step 2C	10 Step 3A Step 3B	11 Step 3C	12	13 Step 3D	14
15 Step 4A	16 Step 4B	17	18 Step 4C	19	20 Step 4D Step 4E	21
22	23 Step 5A Step 5B Step 5C	24 Step 5D	25 Step 5E	26	27 Step 5F	28
29 Step 5G	30	1	2 Step 6 DUE DATE	3	4	5

SUMMARY

This chapter addressed some of the challenges that come with a formal, college-level writing assignment or a research paper. Some basic guidelines for how to approach a writing project were offered. You also learned how to use the calendar and task list as tools to plan a writing project in such a way that you have time to read, write, think, proofread, and revise. This will empower you to do your best work and to submit a paper of which you can be proud.

REVIEW QUESTIONS 7.1

Instructions: Following are five true-false statements taken from the information in this chapter. First, try to answer them without looking back at the chapter. Then review the chapter to see how well you did.

Question & Answer	Rationale
Circle True or False for each of the following statements.	**Write an explanation for why each statement is true or false.**
1. Good planning is a key to success in college-level writing. **True or False**	Your Rationale:
2. If you are writing a paper for a psychology class, you will probably be asked to use the MLA guidelines to format your paper. **True or False**	Your Rationale:
3. You should record the tasks associated with writing a college-level paper on your calendar in reverse order (e.g., record last task first and so on). **True or False**	Your Rationale:
4. The chapter compared writing a formal college-level paper to eating a giant pizza because if you take on too much at one time you will get sick. **True or False**	Your Rationale:
5. It is a good idea to quote from the dictionary (and cite it because it adds an extra source to your paper and helps support your argument). **True or False**	Your Rationale:

Name: ______________________

Chapter Seven **Study Guide**

Chapter 7, Goal 1: The student will be able to identify and apply guidelines for writing a college-level paper.

Questions	Answers & Notes

Name: ______________________________

Chapter Seven

Study Guide

Chapter 7, Goal 2: The student will be able to distinguish between peer-reviewed journal articles and other types of literature.

Questions	Answers & Notes

Name: ______________________________

Chapter Seven **Study Guide**

Chapter 7, Goal 3: The student will be able to apply specified style manual rules (such as MLA or APA) to a college-level paper.

Questions	Answers & Notes

Name: ____________________________________

Chapter Seven

Study Guide

Chapter 7, Goal 4: The student will be able to apply basic formatting tips when writing either a general college-level paper or a research paper.

Questions	Answers & Notes

Name: ______________________________

Chapter Seven **Study Guide**

Chapter 7, Goal 5: The student will be able to understand the process (steps) for creating a formal college-level paper.

Questions	Answers & Notes

Name: ______________________________

Chapter Seven

Study Guide

Chapter 7, Goal 6: The student will be able to design a plan for creating a research paper over a reasonable span of time.

Questions	Answers & Notes

Name: ______________________________

Preparing for Class:
Use This Page to Record Questions or Insights to Discuss in Class.

Practice Finding Resources

Goal:

The purpose of this activity is for the student to master using the library to collect resources for a college research paper.

Objective:

The student will demonstrate understanding of how to use the library to retrieve a refereed journal article and how to write a citation for the article in both APA and MLA styles.

Instructions:

In preparation for this assignment, you should review the information from this chapter about how to distinguish a scholarly article from other types of publications and about the APA and MLA style manuals. You will find the "Comparison Chart for MLA, APA, and CMS" very helpful when you write the citation information for the article you retrieve. The comparison chart is available from **http://bvtlab.com/2m85U**.

Once you have prepared by reviewing the items listed above, you should finish this assignment by following these three steps:

Step 1: Determine the topic of your research quest.

Step 2: Log on to your college library website, and conduct a search for a refereed (also called peer-reviewed) article on the topic you chose. Once you find an article, save it as a PDF file so that you can look it over later.

Step 3: Answer the questions about your article in the space provided on the next page. Remember that you can use the OWL to easily figure out how to write the citation.

Practice Finding Resources

Name: ______________________ **Class Section:** __________

Fill in the appropriate information in the space provided on this page.

What topic did you search for?
What is the title of the article that you found?
Write the citation for the article as it would appear in the reference list for an APA paper.
Write the citation for the article as it would appear on the Works Cited page for an MLA paper.
How did you determine that this was a scholarly article? List **several** ways.

Chapter 8 Roadmap

Connecting to Resources: People, Places, and Things

In this chapter you will learn about the on-campus resources that can help make students successful. These resources include people, places, and technologies.

This chapter roadmap page presents the formal learning goals for this chapter and a checklist that you should follow as you read and study the chapter.

Student Learning Goals for This Chapter

After completing this chapter the student should be able to do the following:

1. Understand and effectively use various technologies, including the college website, the college library website, and the college's course management system (Blackboard, WebCT, D2L, etc.).
2. Practice an etiquette that will promote effective communication with professors and others.
3. List and describe what resources are available from the college library, counseling centers, and various offices on campus.
4. Identify, appreciate, cooperate, and coordinate with the various people on campus who can contribute in some way to the student's success.

Checklist for This Chapter

Target date/ deadline	Check when completed	Activity
________	❑	1. Complete Critical Thinking Activity 8.1.
________	❑	2. Convert the learning goals above to questions that you can answer as you read the chapter. Write your questions on the study guide pages near the end of this chapter.
________	❑	3. Read the chapter.
________	❑	4. Try to answer the reading comprehension questions as you come to them in the chapter. Check each answer by comparing it to the list of correct answers in the back of the book. If any answer was not correct, then review the passages preceding the question to see why you missed the question.
________	❑	5. Use the study guide pages near the end of this chapter to answer the questions you created in Step 2. Once completed, these pages will be your study guide.
________	❑	6. Write down any questions, insights, or comments that you have as you read so that you can bring them up in class.
________	❑	7. Complete Review Questions 8.1.
________	❑	8. Complete Assignment 8.1.

CRITICAL THINKING ACTIVITY 8.1

In this chapter you will learn some simple, but important, things that will help you be successful. Consider the following questions. Can you answer all of them without looking up the answers? These are practical things that you need to know as a college student; you are likely to experience situations in which ignorance of these simple things could keep you from being successful.

1. What are four things that you should include in every email message that you send to your professor?

2. Describe what a special collection is in a college library. Why might it be useful to you?

3. What is a course management system, and how does it work?

4. How does your college website work?

Connecting to Resources: People, Places, and Things

8

> *The Internet is becoming the town square for the global village of tomorrow.*
>
> — *Bill Gates*[1]

> *A library is not a luxury but one of the necessities of life.*
>
> — *Henry Ward Beecher*[2]

> *A university is just a group of buildings gathered around a library.*
>
> — *Shelby Foote*[3]

One of the most important things that new students can do to make success in college a reality is to discover and take advantage of the many campus resources available to them. In this chapter we will highlight a few of those resources, which include people, places, and technologies.

Table 8.1 Successful Students Connect to Campus Resources

People	Places	Things
Advisors	Learning Center	College website
Coaches	Computer labs	College email
Counselors	Counseling Center	College catalog
Faculty	Financial Aid Office	Course management system (D2L, Blackboard, etc.)
Grounds and building staff	Fitness Center	Faculty web pages
Librarians	Library	College library site
Office staff	Registrar's Office	Your personal college portal
Other students	Student organizations	
Security	Auditorium	
Academic tutors		

8.1 People

Following are brief descriptions of some of the people on campus that, in some way, contribute to your success as a student. You are literally surrounded by these helpers every day. You will interact often with some of these people, whereas others seem to work behind the scenes. Reading about them in this chapter will encourage you to do the following:

1. Realize that they are there, working every day, ultimately for your benefit.
2. Cooperate with them in their efforts.
3. Take advantage of the service that they offer to you.
4. Show appreciation for what they do.

Advisors

An academic advisor is someone assigned to help you develop a class schedule, register for classes, develop your short- and long-range plans and explain the degree program requirements to you, assist you with dropping or adding classes, and answer specific questions that you may have about your program of study. Check with your academic department or division to find out the name of your advisor. Some colleges have an advisement center with full time employees devoted entirely to advisement. You would be wise to seek their advice. Sometimes students are inclined to take the advice of other students on these matters. Be careful because some rules or policies change from year to year. Your student friends might not be aware of changes to programs, prerequisites, and so on; your advisor, however, will know the most accurate information.

Coaches

Coaches head athletic teams and serve student athletes in many ways. If you take the time to talk to any one of them, you will quickly discover that they are not concerned merely with the success of the team (winning games) but that they also strive to help the students under their leadership to develop and to succeed academically.

Counselors

The vast majority of colleges provide a counseling office or counseling center of some type. Counselors can help with a variety of personal issues, disability issues, and issues with the transition to college. Keep in mind that counseling is not just for those with special problems; rather, counseling is beneficial to all students. The services that most counseling centers offer are described in detail later in this chapter.

Faculty (Office Hours)

Of course, in class you interact with instructors several times a week—but don't forget about office hours. As has already been mentioned, each faculty member has designated certain hours during the week during which he or she plans to be in the office so that students can visit and receive assistance. If you need help with a course, you should not hesitate to make an appointment to visit with your instructor. It is easy to find out when these office hours are because they are usually listed in the syllabus and posted on each faculty member's office door. Usually, the department or division secretaries also have a list of the office hours for everyone in the division. You will find that faculty members are very busy with research, writing, paperwork, grading, committee meetings, and so on. However, you should also know this: helping students is a top priority for college faculty.

Staff

Before most students are even awake, the grounds and building crews are already hard at work at your college making the grounds and buildings beautiful, comfortable, and accessible to students. The food service staff arrives early and starts preparing to serve the campus community. Much of what we do on campus would come to a screeching halt were it not for the long-suffering labor of the computer services staff working, mostly behind the scenes, to keeping everything running. Secretaries and other office staff spend many hours each day helping students connect with the right people, fill out the correct forms, and solve other problems. All of these people take pride in the fact that they are there to help you. You should demonstrate gratitude and cooperate with them whenever possible because, after all, you are helping them help you.

Librarians

A library is not merely a hollow room lined with books; it is, instead, a hive of information driven by a staff that works diligently to design, manage, and continually update the library as a resource for students. Most students would earn much higher grades and get a lot more out of college if they used the library more. The library staff is ready to help you do just that. The library staff can help you understand the library and make use of its resources. Using the library will help you with classroom assignments and papers. Additional information about the library appears later in this chapter.

Other Students

One of the best resources available to you in college is other students. People are greatly influenced by the groups to which they belong. That is why it is very important that you make meaningful connections to other students who care about success in college as much as you do. Your grandmother was correct when she advised you to avoid friends who just want to party all the time, waste time goofing off instead of studying, and participate in nefarious activities like excessive alcohol and drug use. You need to find partners in each of your classes who can help you study for that class and fill you in on what you need to know if you ever have to miss a class. Seek out student organizations that reflect both your interests and your anticipated career. Student clubs should not take away from your study time; but in proper balance they can offer you networking opportunities, orient you to the norms of your chosen career, help you develop valuable work-related and communication skills, and provide you with opportunities to simply have fun. Your college website probably has a page or area devoted to various clubs and student organizations, and you should look into them as soon as you can. Table 8.2 provides just a few examples of typical student organizations and clubs you might find in college.

Table 8.2 Examples of Student Organizations

African-American Union	The Robert Feline Playmakers (theater)
Alpha Sigma Psi (Anthropology, Sociology, & Psychology club)	SGA (Student Government Association)
Art Mania Club	SIFE (Students in Free Enterprise)
Chess Club	SNEA (Student National Education Association)
EARTH Club	Tennis Club
International Club	STEMMEGA (Math and Science Club)
Music Makers Club	Video Gamers Association

Security

Campus security personnel are not there merely to give you a parking ticket if you park in a restricted zone. Campus police work around the clock, keeping a watchful eye in order to protect you. Help them serve you better by cooperating with posted speed limits and other laws and by reporting emergencies or suspicious activities to them. If an emergency situation, such as a natural disaster or school shooting, occurs on your campus, campus security are likely to be the first on the scene. Cooperate with them and follow their instructions because that may just save your life.

Academic Tutors

Some of the most appreciated helpers on campus are the academic tutors who work in learning centers. These tutors help students with math and writing challenges. You will be surprised how much easier success will come if you visit your college's learning center. Few students realize what a huge benefit it is when tutors are provided on your campus for free (or included as a part of your regular student fees). If tutors were not provided, and you found yourself seeking the services of a private tutor, you would most likely pay a hefty price for the service.

Years ago, one of my students lamented to me that she had failed a required beginning level math course twice. She said, "I fear that I will never be able to graduate because I can't get past this required math class, and I just can't understand Professor Smith." The student had good grades in her other classes. When I looked at her schedule, I noticed that she had a free hour after her math class and that the tutoring lab was in the same building as her math classroom. I suggested that she simply go to the tutoring lab after each math class, sit in the lab and do her math homework. Then if she came upon a problem that she did not know how to solve, she could ask a tutor to explain it. In this way she could learn the parts of the math lesson that she had difficulty with one problem at a time, and she would never fall behind in class. She followed my advice. During the next semester, she stopped me in the hall one day to tell me, with excitement, that the plan had worked and that she had earned an A. That student learned just how valuable the campus tutoring service can be.

8.2 Places

Following are brief descriptions of some of the places on most campuses that, in some way, contribute to your success as a student. This is not an exhaustive list. It is a bit humbling to realize that the entire campus infrastructure exists to help you as a student. A lot has been invested in your success.

Learning Centers or Academic Centers

These can be some of the most important locations on campus because centers often provide free tutoring for English, math, and other subjects. Try to visit your college's learning center as soon as you can during the semester to acquaint yourself with all that the center has to offer. Take note of the contact information, such as the telephone number, email address, and web address, and of the hours of operation. Then, return any time you need help.

Computer Labs

Computer labs are located in various buildings across most campuses. Students should make a note of which computer labs are located near them and what times those labs are open. Wireless Internet access is also available on most campuses for students who wish to use their own laptop computers, tablet computers, or other wireless devices. Check the college web page or the IT department to find out how to connect.

Counseling Center

Counseling centers exist to enable students to achieve their goals and reach their fullest potential by offering personal, career, and academic counseling services. Many colleges offer individual and group therapies, stress management seminars, and other types of psychologically educational seminars throughout the year as well. Table 8.3 shows some of the services that counseling centers typically offer. Do not hesitate to use their services when you need help.

Table 8.3 Services Offered by Most Counseling Centers (CCs)

Service	Description
Personal Counseling	CCs can help you cope with life changes (relationships, adjustment to college, relocation), and with personal problems (stress management, depression, test anxiety).
Career Counseling	Most CCs offer a Career Resource Library and a computerized career guidance program. They can provide access to information about occupations, schools, financial aid, and job-seeking resources. They can also help you 1) assess your career interest, abilities, and job values; 2) explore occupations, majors, and schools; and 3) develop a resume and conduct a job search.
Academic Counseling	Academic counseling includes assessment of your learning style, counseling on test preparation techniques, and counseling on test anxiety.
Disability Services	This service is provided for students who need help with classroom accommodations due to a disability.
Outreach Programs	Upon request, most CCs will provide workshops on stress management, test anxiety, eating disorders, sexual assault awareness and prevention, time management, depression, diversity awareness, communication, and so on.
Group Counseling	Assertiveness training, test anxiety, stress management, single parenthood, healthy relationships, nontraditional student support—all are topics covered in group counseling.
Consultation Services	Most CCs will also meet with individuals, small groups, organizations, and departments to assist them in defining issues and developing strategies to deal with concerns.

Most colleges have a webpage for the Counseling Center that offers links and information on a wide variety of issues. Table 8.4 shows some of the topics that might be addressed by your college CC webpage. Take time to browse your college's CC webpage so that you will be aware of what resources are available to you when you need them.

Table 8.4 Topics Addressed by Many CC Websites

Topics
Accommodations for disabilities policy
Career resources
Crisis intervention protocol
Conflict resolution and mediation
De-escalation presentation
Disability resources
Disability services manual
Mental health
Confidentiality statement
Self help

The Library

This chapter began with an engaging quote by Shelby Foote that expresses the prominence of the library on campus: "A university is just a group of buildings gathered around a library."[2] If the library were a person, she might appear to the casual observer to be quiet and unassuming; yet to the serious college student, the library is revealed as an incredible hulk of academic power.

Students on college campuses can access thousands of books, journal articles, and other resources online through their library. To make the most effective use of the library during your time in college, you need to understand how it is organized, what resources are offered, and what policies are in effect.

Organization

In most colleges and universities, the books in the library are arranged on the shelves according to the Library of Congress Classification System, which separates all knowledge into twenty-one classes. Each class is identified by a letter of the alphabet, subclasses by combination of letters, and subtopics within classes and subclasses by a numerical notation.

Locating Materials and Information

In most libraries, there are computer labs that provide all of the information you need to locate books, videos, periodicals, and thousands of other resources. In many cases you can search the holdings of the library online. Libraries provide services to link students to thousands of reference materials that will assist you in being successful in your college studies. Usually, libraries have a main hub that provides access to multiple databases, which in turn hold thousands of articles in periodicals and chapters in books. Many articles are full text. Students who need periodical articles that are not available in their library can often obtain those materials through an interlibrary loan system. Ask the library staff about requesting materials.

Research Help

A series of studies called the ERIAL (Ethnographic Research in Illinois Academic Libraries) project found that many students, even when they struggled to find good sources, did not seek help from the librarians.[4] These studies also found that students who had attended library orientations or tutorials showed more proficiency than those who had not.[4] You will be more successful in college if you attend library orientations and make it a point to ask the librarians for help when you need it.

Most librarians have created subject-specific research guides and course-specific guides to help you with any research project you may have. These guides are crafted to help you when you do not know where to begin your research in a certain subject area or are produced to help you with a specific course. Be sure to ask your librarian about any library guides that might be available to you.

Atmosphere

College libraries strive to accommodate both group and individual study. They often have several, small study rooms available for group study. There are usually collaborative study areas, as well as quiet areas to study alone. These provide nice places to study if your home environment is noisy or distracting (as is often the case for students who live in dorms or shared apartments). If you ever need help accessing any of these study areas in the library, a library staff member will be happy to assist you.

Special Collections

Most campus libraries house special collections about specific topics or people. These collections can house print items, images, manuscripts, maps, artifacts, microforms, and digital and audio-visual materials. Many of these collections relate to the specific college, local history, regional and state history, and genealogy. As such, collections typically include many items that are unique, historical, rare, and/or irreplaceable.

Reading Comprehension Question 8.1 (Knowledge)

How are the books in the library arranged?

a. In alphabetical order by title
b. In groups and categories, according to the Dewey Decimal System
c. In accordance with the Library of Congress Classification System
d. In no particular order at all

The Campus Bus System

(It is not a place, but your campus bus system will *take you* places.) Forrest Gump's mama told him that a good pair of shoes could take him anywhere. If Forrest were a student in college, however, he might appreciate knowing that many colleges have a campus bus system that would take him places faster.

In order to reach some locations, you may have to transfer from one route to the other. You should check the bus schedules and include that information in your calendar planner. If you can, plan how you get to and from classes *before* you register for them and certainly before the semester gets underway.

8.3 Technology

Internet technologies are now ubiquitous in higher education, but which technologies and which practices are most likely to help you be successful in college? What practices might thwart your success? How is your use of technology for success in college different from the use of technology in other capacities?

This chapter addresses electronic technologies and physical resources that will help you to be successful in college. Simply knowing how to use these programs is not enough to make you successful. You must know how to use them effectively in the college environment. There will be times that you need to turn technology off so that you can spend time thinking and focusing exclusively on your studies.

Your College Portal

Some colleges have a web portal that you will be able to use to access many resources online. In this case, you would log on to the web portal with a username and password. Once you have logged on, you may have access to a number of different accounts: your campus email account, your campus financial account, your campus records, and/or your campus course delivery system. If you do not know your username or password, be sure to ask a staff or faculty member how to access your college's web portal. You will find that, usually, there is a "forgot your username" or "forgot you password" link on the website, so you may wish to check that first.

College Webmail

The vast majority of colleges have an email program similar to Hotmail or Gmail. It is very important to check your college webmail on a regular basis since it is usually the official email system of your college—the method by which information and important announcements will be delivered to you throughout the semester and your career at college. Look for links regarding webmail on the college home page. (Sometimes, there is an option to have your college email forwarded to your personal email address—but you should still log on to your college email periodically to clean out your inbox so there is enough room for new messages.)

Anatomy of an Email to Your Professor

Email messages that you send to your professor, or to other college staff, should not be as casual in style and content as those messages that you might send to a friend. Your professor may teach hundreds of students in five or more classes. Therefore, when you send an email to the professor, it is very important that you identify yourself and indicate specifically which class you are taking.

Be sure to use the following guidelines every time you write to a professor:

1. Always include your full name as part of the message.
2. Always identify about which class you are writing. Specify the name of the class (e.g., SOC 1101 Sociology), and the section (e.g., Section B), and class meeting particulars (e.g., meeting TH at 9:30 a.m.).
3. Always include your contact information (such as your email address and/or phone number) so that the professor may respond to your message if necessary.

4. Always use complete sentences and correct grammar.

Following are three examples of email messages: one that has the correct characteristics and two that do not and are not appropriate. The names have been changed to protect the innocent (or guilty), but these are *actual emails* that have been received from students. Can you identify what is wrong with the poorly written messages? How many problems can you find in the poorly written messages?

Reading Comprehension Question 8.2 (Literal Comprehension)

Which of the following is true according to this chapter?

a. Emails to a professor should always identify you by your name and your class and should include your contact information.
b. Emails to a professor are very similar to texting, except that you may have to use the college webmail system to deliver them.
c. Emails to your professor should be casual and friendly.
d. Emails sent through the campus webmail system automatically identify you and provide your contact information, so you do not need to do so.

Example of a Really, Truly, Undeniably Horrible Email Message

From:	Christobel@hotmail.com
Date:	3/11/2014 11:18:29 am
To:	bsmith@uga.edu
Subject:	(no subject)
Attachments:	

wht up when is r test

Example of a Poorly Composed Email Message

From:	Christobel@hotmail.com
Date:	3/11/2014 11:18:29 am
To:	bsmith@uga.edu
Subject:	Test Date
Attachments:	

When is our next test?
Chris

Example of a Well-Written Email Message

From:	cgriffin3@uga.edu
Date:	3/11/2014 11:18:29 am
To:	bsmith@uga.edu
Subject:	Social Problems Assignment from Chris Griffin
Attachments:	Chris_Griffin_Assignment1.doc (112 k)

Professor Smith,

Per your instructions in the syllabus, I have attached writing assignment #1 for Social Problems (Section B, 12:30 pm, MW) to this email.

Please send a reply to confirm that you have received it as I do not wish for the assignment to be late.

Sincerely,

Chris Griffin

cgriffin3@ega.edu

478-455-4123

Things You Should Know About Most College Webmail

There are usually links on your college's home page from which you can discover the webmail addresses and telephone numbers of your professors, advisor, and staff members for the various departments and offices on campus.

You can usually locate policies regarding your college's webmail on the college website. You should make sure that you are aware of those policies. If your college, like many, sends important college correspondence to your college webmail account instead of using paper mail (snail mail) or any other email accounts that you may have, then it is vital that you check your college webmail on a regular basis.

Reading Comprehension Question 8.3 (Inferential Comprehension)

What is the main idea of the passage above entitled, "Things You Should Know About Most College Webmail"?

a. Webmail has certain policies and established norms about the correct and incorrect way to use webmail in college.

b. Webmail is very complicated and difficult to learn.

c. Webmail can be used to publicize a personal business.

d. None of the above

Course Management Systems

A course management system (CMS) or learning management system (LMS) is a software program that your college uses to manage online courses or the online components of face-to-face (F2F) courses. Examples of course management systems include Blackboard, Desire 2 Learn (D2L), Moodle, and Angel. There are others. Your college may use one of these, a different CMS, or one of these called by a name unique to your institution.

The CMS is used to deliver online courses and hybrid courses (courses that meet partly online and partly in a classroom) and to enhance F2F classes. Even if you are not enrolled in an online or hybrid course, your professor may use the CMS to post information for your class, such as the syllabus or grades. In some cases the professor of an F2F class may use a CMS for much more—such as email, discussions, quizzes, surveys, handouts, instructional videos, calendar, announcements, and so on. Ask your professor about this at the beginning of the semester so that you will know what to expect and so that you will not miss out on any resources that might help you succeed in the course. Look for tutorials on the college website to help you learn to navigate your college's particular CMS.

It would be wise to check your college webpage for the technical requirements of the CMS *before* you get started accessing your courses online because you may need to adjust your computer or use certain programs on your computer to make it compatible with the CMS used at your college. For example, the CMS may not work properly in all Internet browsers and may specify which browsers or versions of particular browsers you should use. Examples of browsers include Google Chrome, Firefox, and Safari, to name a few. Also, the CMS may require that you set your browser to allow cookies, pop-ups, and/or JavaScript. Some of the courses that you access through the CMS may also require plug-ins, such as Adobe Reader, Adobe Flash Player, QuickTime Player, and/or Windows Media Player for your browser.

Using Your College Database Software

Colleges often use database software systems for administrative applications. Your college database software program is probably connected to the database where student enrollment and grade information is stored. Usually, you can access your college's database software program from the college home page. You should find out what your college's software database program is called (for example, BANNER or WINGS) so that you can make full use of the system. As a student, you can usually use your college database software to manage many aspects of your college experience. Following are examples of some of the things for which you can usually use your college database software:

- You can check your own records at the college—such as registration status, financial aid status, and registration holds.
- You can view the course schedule for the current and future semesters.
- You may be able to register yourself for classes online.
- You may be able to check your midterm grades.
- You can view your official grades at the end of the semester.

Reading Comprehension Question 8.4 (Analysis)

What is the primary purpose of the parts of this chapter dealing with technology?

a. To show the student how advanced the technology is at college

b. To demonstrate to the student that there are rules about using email in college

c. To assist the student in becoming familiar with various internet technologies in order to increase the student's chances for success in college

d. To point out the deficiencies in college internet technologies

Want to learn more?

Try these resources.

"See You Online! Tips for Using College Library Resources and the Web"
http://bvtlab.com/68JBN
The *Back to College®* website presents this article by Sylvia DeSantis in which she describes college and university online databases, using search engines for college research and university electronic catalogs.

Library Survival Skills for New College Students:
http://bvtlab.com/rXne8
This webpage, prepared by Nancy Guidry and Dawn Dobie of the Bakersfield College Library, presents and describes fourteen library skills that new students need to succeed.

"Top 10 Ways Your College Library Can Help You"
http://bvtlab.com/r2aUW
This short article by Courtney Brunch appears in the *Front Range Community College Blog: Writing the Front Range* and lists ten ways that the college library can help students.

Summary

This chapter discussed many of the people, places, and technologies that will help you succeed in college. People include advisors, coaches, counselors, faculty, buildings and grounds staff, librarians, office staff, security and other students. Places include learning centers, computer labs, counseling centers, financial aid offices, fitness centers, libraries, registrar's offices and student organizations. With regard to technology, you learned some basic information about your college's webmail, course management system, and college database software systems. A simple—but very important—topic of this chapter was the discussion of the anatomy of an email to your professor. If you make the extra effort to make sure that your email messages have the characteristics described in this chapter, you will enjoy much more successful communication with your professors. Improving your communication skills will contribute to your overall success in college and your subsequent career.

Review Questions

8.1

Instructions: Following are five true-false statements taken from the information in this chapter. First, try to answer them without looking back at the chapter. Then review the chapter to see how well you did.

Question & Answer	Rationale
Circle true or false for each of the following statements.	**Write an explanation stating why each statement is true or false.**
1. Students should always use Gmail to check their official college mailbox. **True or False**	Your Rationale:
2. Using your college's database software program is important because it will allow you to access your grades and progress in college. **True or False**	Your Rationale:
3. Counseling centers help with a very limited number of psychological issues for college students. **True or False**	Your Rationale:
4. When sending an email message to a professor via webmail, there is no need to mention the class about which you are writing. **True or False**	Your Rationale:
5. If the library were a person, she might appear to the casual observer to be quiet and unassuming; however, to the serious college student, the library is revealed as an incredible hulk of academic power. **True or False**	Your Rationale:

Name: ______________________________

Chapter Eight **Study Guide**

Chapter 8, Goal 1: The student will be able to effectively use various technologies, including the college website, the college library website, and the college's course management system (Blackboard, WebCT, D2L, etc.).

Questions	Answers & Notes

Name: ______________________

Chapter Eight **Study Guide**

Chapter 8, Goal 2: The student will be able to practice an etiquette that will promote effective communication with professors and others.

Questions	Answers & Notes

Name: ____________________

Chapter Eight

Study Guide

Chapter 8, Goal 3: The student will be able to list and describe what resources are available from his or her college library, counseling centers, learning centers, and other offices on campus.

Questions	Answers & Notes

Name: ______________________________

Chapter Eight **Study Guide**

Chapter 8, Goal 4: The student will be able to identify, appreciate, cooperate, and coordinate with the various people on campus who contribute, in some way, to the student's success.

Questions	Answers & Notes

Name: ______________________

Preparing for Class:
Use This Page to Record Questions or Insights to Discuss in Class.

Assignment 8.1

Identifying Campus Resources

Instructions:

This assessment provides you with a worksheet to help you to identify campus resources and to always be prepared to take advantage of their services.

Step 1: Use the form on the following pages to record some information about the different resources available on your campus. Examples of resources include the library, your academic advisor, the tutoring center, computer labs, faculty and teaching assistants, departmental offices for your major, coaches, and so on. The information should include contact information, office hours or hours of operation, location, and how the resource can help you. Record the information in the space provided.

Step 2: Insert or copy these pages into your calendar/planner so that you will always have the information when you need it. If you use an electronic calendar/planner, then copy the information to your electronic planner so that you will have access to it when you need it. Remember to update the information any time the details, such as hours of operation, change.

Notes

Assignment 8.1

Directory of Campus Resources

Resource:	How can this resource help you?
Phone/Fax:	
Email:	
Webpage:	
Location:	
Hours of Operation:	

Resource:	How can this resource help you?
Phone/Fax:	
Email:	
Webpage:	
Location:	
Hours of Operation:	

Resource:	How can this resource help you?
Phone/Fax:	
Email:	
Webpage:	
Location:	
Hours of Operation:	

Resource:	How can this resource help you?
Phone/Fax:	
Email:	
Webpage:	
Location:	
Hours of Operation:	

Resource:	How can this resource help you?
Phone/Fax:	
Email:	
Webpage:	
Location:	
Hours of Operation:	

(continues)

Assignment 8.1

Directory of Campus Resources *(continued)*

Resource:	How can this resource help you?
Phone/Fax:	
Email:	
Webpage:	
Location:	
Hours of Operation:	

Resource:	How can this resource help you?
Phone/Fax:	
Email:	
Webpage:	
Location:	
Hours of Operation:	

Resource:	How can this resource help you?
Phone/Fax:	
Email:	
Webpage:	
Location:	
Hours of Operation:	

Resource:	How can this resource help you?
Phone/Fax:	
Email:	
Webpage:	
Location:	
Hours of Operation:	

Resource:	How can this resource help you?
Phone/Fax:	
Email:	
Webpage:	
Location:	
Hours of Operation:	

Chapter 9 Roadmap

Balancing College Life: Walking the Tightrope

It is often a difficult transition from home to college, in that you must now learn how to balance all the responsibilities—academic, psychological, physical, and financial—of your life entirely (or mostly) on your own. This chapter will provide some tips on managing your life during the first year of college.

This chapter roadmap page presents the formal learning goals for this chapter and a checklist that you should follow as you read and study the chapter.

Student Learning Goals for This Chapter

After completing this chapter the student should be able to do the following:

1. Define balance and list four important elements of balance in life at college.
2. Describe the characteristics of a college student who maintains balance in his or her life during college.
3. Discuss at least five ways to maintain academic balance in the first year of college.
4. Discuss at least five ways to maintain psychological balance in the first year of college.
5. Discuss at least five ways to maintain physical balance in the first year of college.
6. Discuss at least five ways to maintain financial balance in the first year of college.

Checklist for This Chapter

Target date/ deadline	Check when completed	Activity
________	❑	1. Complete Critical Thinking Activity 9.1.
________	❑	2. Convert the learning goals above to questions that you can answer as you read the chapter. Write your questions on the study guide pages near the end of this chapter.
________	❑	3. Read the chapter.
________	❑	4. Try to answer the reading comprehension questions as you come to them in the chapter. Check each answer by comparing it to the list of correct answers in the back of the book. If any answer was not correct, then review the passages preceding the question to see why you missed the question.
________	❑	5. Use the study guide pages near the end of this chapter to answer the questions you created in Step 2. Once completed, these pages will be your study guide.
________	❑	6. Write down any questions, insights, or comments that you have as you read so that you can bring them up in class (if applicable).
________	❑	7. Complete Review Questions 9.1.
________	❑	8. Complete Assignment 9.1.

CRITICAL THINKING ACTIVITY 9.1

Before you read this chapter and without looking up any information about the topic on the Internet or elsewhere, use the space provided on this page to write your answers to the following questions:

1. When you think of balance, what comes to your mind? Write your thoughts below.

2. What do you think Gordon B. Hinckley meant in the following quote?

> *"The major work of the world is not done by geniuses. It is done by ordinary people, with balance in their lives, who have learned to work in an extraordinary manner."*
>
> *— Gordon B. Hinckley*[3]

3. Think of ways in which your life could become out of balance during your first year of college. List two ways in which you might ensure that this does not happen:

Balancing College Life:
Walking the Tightrope

9

My point is, life is about balance. The good and the bad. The highs and the lows. The pina and the colada.

Ellen DeGeneres, "Seriously … I'm Kidding"[1]

Mathematics expresses values that reflect the cosmos, including orderliness, balance, harmony, logic, and abstract beauty.

Deepak Chopra[2]

The major work of the world is not done by geniuses. It is done by ordinary people, with balance in their lives, who have learned to work in an extraordinary manner.

Gordon B. Hinckley[3]

Life is like riding a bicycle. To keep your balance, you must keep moving.

Albert Einstein[4]

9.1 Balance Defined

Balance could be defined as a state in which you are meeting all of your obligations to yourself and others. Some people might use the term *equilibrium* to denote a state of balance. Having balance in your life also implies that you feel things are under control. Balance is an elusive concept, however. Each person might define *balance* in life differently. At the core, being balanced means that you are doing the things that you need to do to keep yourself in the most stress-free and healthy environment that you possibly can. It does not mean that you have no stress—nor does it mean, necessarily, that you have no illnesses or diseases. As a college student, achieving balance could be described as maintaining some sort of equilibrium in four main areas: academic, psychological, physical, and financial.

9.2 Elements of Balance in College

Academic

Academic balance can be described as a state in which you are meeting the requirements of all of your courses and are passing them. As we have discussed throughout this textbook, passing means that you are actively learning the information that you need to learn in order to progress in college. Achieving balance in your academic life includes understanding material in each course you are taking, planning for each course, and executing the requirements for each course successfully. Hopefully, this book has given you information that will help you to stay in academic balance.

Psychological

Psychological balance might be described as a state in which you think, feel, and behave in ways that are helpful to you in achieving your goals in life. It means that you are able to complete your daily living activities (such as bathing, dressing, eating) and that you feel a sense of well-being most days. Everyone has times during which they feel "down," sad, or anxious. However, if you are in psychological balance, these times are fleeting; they do not last, and you can behave in ways or do things that will improve those kinds of feelings. Later in the chapter, we will discuss some ideas about what happens when these feelings become pervasive and color most of your days.

Physical

Physical balance is a state in which your physical body is in equilibrium. It does not necessarily mean you have no illness or disease. It does mean, however, that you have your illness **or** disease under control. For example, someone with diabetes could still be physically balanced if he or she is managing the diabetes with proper diet and medication. The person would be out of balance if his or her diet, medication, or stress level caused a drastic increase or decrease in blood sugar, however. If it is midterm week and you get the flu, your body is likely to be out of physical balance. So sometimes we cannot control whether or not we are in balance physically; yet there are many things we can do to help ourselves to stay in physical balance—such as incorporating healthy diet and exercise into our routine, to name but two.

Financial

Financial balance is important for the college student because college is expensive. Financial balance would be a situation in which the student is able to pay for college bills as well as cost-of-living bills. There are many instances in which the parents, relatives, or friends of an individual might help the student pay bills. However, many times the student alone is responsible for paying for educational as well as living expenses. In this case, finances can be stressful, and it is important to pay attention to whether or not you are in financial balance.

Figure 9.1 Four Elements of a Balanced College Student

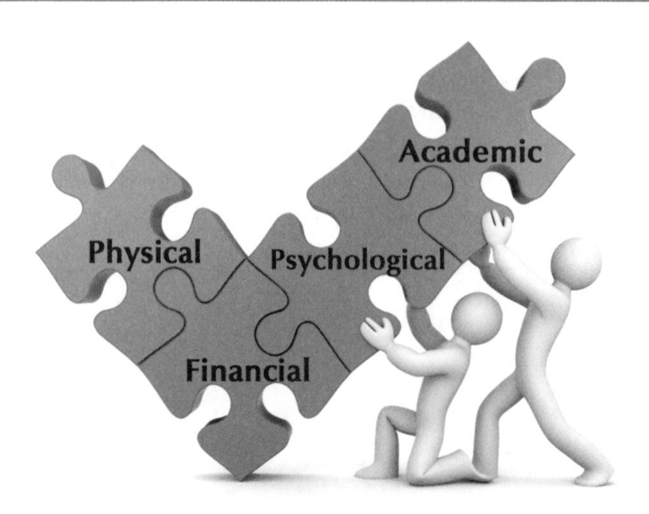

Reading Comprehension Question 9.1 (Knowledge)

In college, it is important to maintain balance in which of the following areas?

a. Financial
b. Academic
c. Psychological
d. Physical
e. All of the above

9.3 Characteristics of a Balanced College Student

We have discussed four characteristics that contribute to a student being balanced (see Figure 9.1). A balanced college student is one who is learning what is needed to pass all his or her college courses, feels and behaves in ways that facilitate his or her life goals, has a body that is in equilibrium, and is able to pay for college and cost-of-living bills. Balance does not necessarily imply perfection. Stress is an inevitable part of life and people feel stressed under many life circumstances, including college. However, balance implies that, given your life circumstances, you are able to get through your daily activities and have a sense of well-being about your life in general.

During certain times in our lives, we have all experienced a lack of balance. It is not a good feeling. When we do not have balance, we are more susceptible to physical and psychological illnesses, and we may experience extreme levels of stress. During college, you are no exception. Being healthy means that you monitor your own body and mind and that you are aware of the things that contribute to being in or out of balance. When you do that, you will be better able to conduct yourself in ways that maintain balance as opposed to ways that cause disruption.

The next section discusses ways in which you can maintain balance in academic, financial, psychological, and physical areas during your college years.

9.4 Ways to Maintain Balance

Academic Balance

This book provides the tools that you need to maintain academic balance. By reading and completing activities in the book, you should have learned many techniques (including the following) that are designed to help you learn and to be successful in college:

1. Understanding how college is different from high school
2. Learning how to organize your materials and courses
3. Connecting with campus resources that can help you be successful
4. Planning ahead so that you can be sure to accomplish all your goals
5. Knowing the importance of learning and your learning style
6. Using appropriate techniques for reading, listening, and writing in college
7. Maintaining your commitment to your time management schedule, in spite of new social freedoms and the attraction of time bandits

These techniques are by no means the only ways you can maintain academic balance. The websites below are dependable and provide really good information about maintaining academic balance during your time as a college student.

For further information:

The following University of Florida website discusses ways to cope with problems, how to recognize signs of distress in yourself and others, and the differences between effective and ineffective coping in college:
http://bvtlab.com/md8qr

The University of British Columbia has a page that discusses procrastination, time management, stressors, and relaxation:
http://bvtlab.com/D4u33

Psychological Balance

Maintaining psychological balance includes the following:

1. Engaging in behaviors that reduce your level of stress
2. Using social support networks to help when you are feeling out of balance
3. Behaving in ways that contribute to a sense of daily well-being
4. Thinking in ways that support your accomplishment of life goals
5. Being able to maintain your daily activities
6. Having friendships and relationships that are supportive to your goals

Common Psychological Issues Experienced by College Students

Depression

Feeling sad is common among college freshmen. Sadness occurs when you feel a loss in your life. Moving to college—away from all your friends, family, and familiar support systems—can cause feelings of grief and loss for anyone. Sadness can sometimes be accompanied by a loss of (or excessive) sleep, a change in appetite, a change in libido, and an inability to feel happy about anything, manifested through frequent crying and other symptoms.

Remember these important ways to help yourself when you are feeling sad:

1. Do things that make you feel better during the day.
2. Assess the level of sadness you are experiencing.
3. Seek help if your sadness persists or if it causes you to change your daily behaviors—such as to miss classes, to stay in bed, to take drugs or drink alcohol excessively, or to avoid doing things with friends.

Almost all colleges have a counseling center that provides individual and group help for students who are experiencing sadness. Seek out help from your counseling center if you are unsure about your level of sadness, or if you know that you are feeling depressed. *Don't wait too long, because there are treatments that can help you before your depression begins to affect your daily activities and grades.*

This chapter is not designed to provide treatment for depression. The very best way to handle the sadness or depression that you might be feeling is to go to the college counseling center where you can talk with someone who can assess your level of depression, and provide therapy (or medication) if needed.

There are many instances in which you might think one of your college friends is depressed. You might notice a change in your friend's appearance, attitude, and behaviors. Sometimes college students who are depressed will talk about suicide or some way of getting out of their situation. This is an emergency. *You need to call 911 if your friend is in imminent danger, or get your friend to the college's counseling center as soon as possible.* Don't ever hesitate to use counseling services on campus—they are a wonderful resource for you while you are in college.

In regard to self help, the following websites are reliable, helpful, and useful if you feel you may be experiencing depression in college or if you are concerned about a friend who is depressed:

For further information:

This excellent webpage from the National Institute of Mental Health (NIMH) deals with answers to frequently asked questions about college depression—such as what depression is and how it affects college students, and different types of depression, including signs and symptoms, causes, and treatments:
http://bvtlab.com/n83J4

This NIMH website also discusses causes, types of depression, diagnosis of depression, signs and symptoms, treatments, and ideas about how to help others who may be depressed:
http://bvtlab.com/dS267

This NIMH online pamphlet answers college students' frequently asked questions about depression. It presents information in a user-friendly manner and includes all you need to know about the illness of depression as well as how to help a friend who may be depressed:
http://bvtlab.com/8d28Q

Am I depressed?
The Anxiety and Depression Association of America (ADAA) has a website that discusses screening for depression and presents a brief screening tool that can be printed to take to your healthcare professional:
http://bvtlab.com/ENghv

Do I have a mental health issue right now?
This website from Mental Health America provides an "M3" screening that tests for depression, anxiety, bipolar disorder, and post traumatic stress disorder. The screening tool provides you with a number that will help you and your doctor understand if you have a treatable mental health disorder. The assessment report that you get when you have completed the M3 provides a scale indicating how disruptive your symptoms are, your risk for various disorders, as well as a section on recommended action. The assessment can either be printed or can be emailed to you.
http://bvtlab.com/6hu68

Stress

Stress is the body's reaction to things that have the potential to harm you. When you enter a brand-new environment, such as college, your body naturally reacts by invoking the stress response. The key is whether you can do things that will turn off this natural stress response, or whether the stress response becomes chronic, or lasting, which can be unhealthy for you. The stress response causes your body to secrete stress hormones and causes physical changes (such as an increase in heart rate and blood pressure and feelings of heightened alertness). When you need it (such as when being attacked by a bear!), this response can save your life. When it happens in a situation that is not life threatening—and when it does not turn off—you might begin to experience health problems as a consequence.

For further information:

This website comes from Harvard Health Publications at Harvard Medical School. It describes how your brain responds to stress as well as ways in which you can take control of your stress:
http://bvtlab.com/3aF77

Just the act of going to college plunges you into a new world in which everything has changed. There are many things that cause college stress, including new classes, new demands and responsibilities, new roles, and new living arrangements—including dealing with a new roommate. It is critical that you recognize when you are stressed and that you do things to reduce your stress level so that it does not become chronic.

For further information:

This website is brought to you by the Nemours Center for Children's Health Media, a part of The Nemours Foundation, a nonprofit organization created by philanthropist Alfred I. du Pont in 1936 and devoted to improving the health of children. This site offers practical and helpful information about seeking and selecting a roommate, about the importance of communication, about day-to-day issues, and about problem-solving with a roommate. You can either read or listen to the article:
http://bvtlab.com/a7khp

This website, also from Nemours, provides an excellent review of stress, causes and signs of stress overload, tips on how to keep your stress under control, and ideas for building your resilience to stress. You can either read or listen to the article:
http://bvtlab.com/K67ku

This website provides ten good tips with practical suggestions about how to deal with stress as a college student. The page is also excellent because it provides many more links to topics that may be of interest to you as you begin your first year of college life:
http://bvtlab.com/a6fZV

Reading Comprehension Question 9.3 (Inferential Comprehension)

What should every college student know about stress?

a. Every college student should know that each body has a specific response to stressful circumstances.

b. Every college student should know that stress can always be controlled.

c. Every college student should know that stress is caused by the individual person.

d. Every college student should know that it is impossible to manage the stresses of college life.

Anxiety

Anxiety is a natural response to stress. Our bodies are designed so that when we are exposed to stressors, we feel anxious or fearful. The way in which you handle the anxiety determines whether or not it will affect your daily activities and goals. Sometimes anxiety can be overwhelming; in some cases, you might even experience panic attacks. If you feel anxious to the point that you are unable to do your required daily activities, you need to seek help immediately. Anxiety can be controlled with therapy and medications, and it is important to get help as soon as you can in order to avoid longer-term problems with your success in college. The following websites might be helpful to you in exploring your own responses to stress and feelings of anxiety:

For further information:

This website from the National Institutes of Mental Health provides a comprehensive booklet about anxiety disorders, covering topics such as symptoms and treatments, ways to get help, and types of anxiety disorders. The booklet can be printed out (since it is provided in .pdf format) or can be ordered free as a hard copy:
http://bvtlab.com/874Gm

This website is brought to you by Medline Plus, a service of the U.S. National Library of Medicine and the National Institutes of Health. The site is unique in that it provides many links to various topics about anxiety. It is essentially a reference page that may be very helpful to you:
http://bvtlab.com/Q8pa8

Do I have an anxiety disorder?
This website from the Anxiety and Depression Association of America has many links to screening tools for disorders such as generalized anxiety disorder, obsessive-compulsive disorder, panic disorder, PTSD, social anxiety disorder, phobias, and depression. The screening tools are arranged so that you can take the screening test, and then print out your results to take to a healthcare professional.
http://bvtlab.com/fPa64

Eating Disorders

Eating disorders are a mental illness—not a choice. Eating disorders include anorexia, bulimia, obesity, and binge eating, and they affect both men and women of college age. Although they are less common in men than in women, they appear to display strikingly similar features in affected individuals of the two genders.[5] The rate of eating disorders among college men ranges from 4 percent to 10 percent, and a recent study on a large university campus found that the female-to-male ratio of positive screens for eating disorder symptoms was 3–1.[6] In samples of adolescent and college students, between 28 percent and 68 percent of normal-weight males perceive themselves as underweight and report a desire to increase their muscle mass through dieting and strength training.[7] One in five women struggle with an eating disorder; of those, 90 percent are between the ages of 12 and 25. Four out of ten people either have an eating disorder or have known someone who does.[8] People with eating disorders also sometimes struggle with other conditions, like chemical dependency, post traumatic stress disorder, sexual abuse, depression, anxiety disorder, morbid obesity, and other problems.[9] If you or a friend is experiencing the symptoms of an eating disorder, seek help immediately. Your college counseling center is a great place to start.

For further information:

The following website comes from the National Association of Anorexia Nervosa and Associated Disorders and covers many eating disorders, including signs and symptoms and true, inspirational stories of recovery:
http://bvtlab.com/676E4

Do I have an eating disorder?
The following website, from the Center for Eating Disorders at Sheppard Pratt, provides a brief online assessment of eating disorders. If your answers suggest that you may have an eating disorder, there is a phone number to call to speak with a member of the Center for Eating Disorders staff, or you can fill out a form to have someone contact you. The site also provides additional links to learn even more about eating disorders.
http://bvtlab.com/7v666

Physical Balance

Striving to maintain balance physically includes several key practices:

1. Eating a diet that is healthy and adequate for you
2. Engaging in exercise that helps you to maintain health
3. Maintaining a healthy perspective on drug and alcohol use
4. Maintaining a healthy sleeping pattern for adequate rest
5. Maintaining healthy practices in sexual and romantic relationships
6. Maintaining health through visiting the doctor when needed

Maintaining a Healthy Diet and Exercising

Keeping your body in good working order includes eating a diet that is healthy for you and that helps you to maintain a body weight that is appropriate for your height, age, and activity level. Exercise should be partnered with a healthy diet. There are thousands of diets out there, and it may be that you have tried a few. However, as you probably know, fad diets rarely lead to healthy or permanent weight loss. Some diets are reasonable, lead to appropriate weight loss, and allow you to keep the weight off over time. If you are the rare person who can eat pretty much whatever you like and still maintain an appropriate body weight, you are lucky. However, even people who are at the right body weight can have a diet that is not necessarily good for them in the long run.

For further information:

This Juvenile Diabetes Research Foundation website offers ten helpful tips for eating healthy in college. It covers how to avoid dietary pitfalls at college as well as how to incorporate healthy eating habits into your college routine.
http://bvtlab.com/79at8

This website from Nemours, *Beating the Freshman Fifteen*, provides information about weight gain during the first year of college, sometimes called "The Freshman Fifteen." It covers how you can avoid gaining weight, including sound approaches to eating and adopting healthy food attitudes. You can either read or listen to the article in audio format.
http://bvtlab.com/6j49j

The following are some trustworthy, well-written websites about maintaining general health in college that offer many ideas about how you can work toward maintaining your health while in your college years.
From the National Institutes of Health:
http://bvtlab.com/3Y95D

From the Centers for Disease Control:
http://bvtlab.com/8637m

Sex and Romance in College

Sex and romance are often part of college life. Students who are between the ages of 18 to 25 are often learning how to date, how to develop romantic relationships, and how to choose an appropriate mate. Perhaps you came to college not having dated very much. Or, maybe you dated throughout high school and are familiar with some of the positive and negative aspects of dating. Contraception and protection from sexually transmitted diseases (STDs) and sexually transmitted infections (STIs) are important and critical issues if you are having sexual relationships in college. Many colleges have contraceptives and other protective devices are available at the Student Health Center. You should make an appointment to visit as soon as possible if you plan on dating. There are many instances in which dating and romantic relationships can interfere with students' daily activities, including studying and attending classes. If you feel you are having problems in school or in life that stem from an issue in a romantic relationship, remember that your counseling center can provide resources that will help you with this issue.

For further information:

This website, *Hot Topics! College Students and Relationships* covers practical issues about what constitutes a "healthy" relationship, how to tell if you may be in an unhealthy relationship, and five steps to setting limits in a relationship: **http://bvtlab.com/9m6w8**

This site, from *Everyday Health* (an email newsletter), is a user-friendly guide to relationships in college and includes decision-making tips about sex in college as well as forms of birth control:
http://bvtlab.com/9dBTN

This website from the American College of Obstetrics and Gynecology answers all the questions you could have about birth control pills:
http://bvtlab.com/6pa78

From the Emerson College Center for Health and Wellness, this site offers information about various types of birth control:
http://bvtlab.com/9NmAt

Sexual identity can also be an issue among college students. Some students struggle with their sexual identity during the time they are attending college. This is a topic that, unfortunately in our society, is sometimes not socially acceptable to discuss freely. Thus, some students find themselves feeling isolated, fearful, and confused about their sexual identity. If these stresses become overwhelming, they can disrupt one's balance and interfere with academic performance. It is important that you seek help if you are struggling with your own sexual identity and that you are sensitive to the fact that new friends you make in college might be struggling with theirs. Remember that your college counseling center usually has resources that can help students with this issue. The following websites might provide some information that can help in this area, too:

For further information:

This website is from the Wright State University Counseling and Wellness Services and discusses self-acknowledgement, disclosure decisions, and research on coming out as a significant experience in college:
http://bvtlab.com/9Aa35

San Jose State University Counseling Services offers this website about gender identity including defining terms, coming out, and navigating your gender identity, as well as a gold mine of resource links to obtain further information and self-help about this topic:
http://bvtlab.com/5n8aP

Drug and Alcohol Use in College

Using alcohol and/or drugs during college is a very common phenomenon. Many students interpret their freedom in college as a chance to do whatever they wish—including the use of drugs and/or alcohol, sometimes in excess. Many students get into trouble with this philosophy. Students who have not been educated on the pitfalls and dangers of alcohol and drug use may get themselves into situations in which their health—even their life—is in serious jeopardy.

If you notice that your drug or alcohol use is affecting the way in which you study or carry out your activities of daily living, you may have a problem. This is not uncommon; your college counseling center can provide services that may help you to understand and deal with college drinking and drug abuse. There are many websites that deal with drug and alcohol use in college. The following websites are trustworthy and have information that can help you to deal with your or a friend's alcohol or drug abuse:

For further information:

This website, created by the National Institute on Alcohol Abuse and Alcoholism (NIAAA), is "your one-stop resource for comprehensive research-based information on issues related to alcohol abuse and binge drinking among college students." It is a comprehensive source of information and links about alcohol use in college. With resources for students, faculty, parents, and others, it is also replete with links to additional information:
http://bvtlab.com/nB2qf

What Peer Educators and Resident Advisors Need to Know about College Drinking is a comprehensive and informative website that includes multiple topics: the scope of the college-drinking problem, the effectiveness of intervention programs currently used by schools and communities, and recommendations for college presidents and researchers on how to improve these interventions and prevention efforts:
http://bvtlab.com/8phb8

The National Institutes on Alcohol Abuse and Alcoholism presents this webpage entitled, "Tips for Cutting Down on Drinking":
http://bvtlab.com/s8867

Do I have a problem with drinking and/or drugs?
There are many screening tests online to assess alcohol and drug use. The following two are brought to you from the National Council on Alcohol and Drug Dependence and are research-based and dependable. When you take the online test, it provides you with a numeric score that is explained, as well as a summary of your test. These materials can also be printed:
http://bvtlab.com/7Q9TV
http://bvtlab.com/f776m

Financial Balance

Maintaining balance in your spending habits during college might make the difference between financial success and financial ruin after college. If you become indebted during college to the extent that you are not able to pay off your loans when you get your first job, it may cause financial difficulties that can persist over many years after you graduate. Therefore, it is critical that you have some information regarding financial stability during college.

One of the great lessons of life is that sooner or later, you will probably need to use credit to purchase something. Many times for students, that becomes a reality when it comes to paying for their college education. Student loans can be the deciding factor in whether or not a student is able to attend a particular college. When student loans are abused or mishandled, however, the problems associated with them can follow you for the rest of your life.

For further information:

The National Endowment for Financial Education has published a booklet entitled, "40 Money Management Tips: What Every College Student Should Know": **http://bvtlab.com/P76bd**

From New York University, this website offers information about understanding the importance of managing your money, establishing credit, and learning how to spend your money wisely:
http://bvtlab.com/s68bK

Reading Comprehension Question 9.2 (Literal Comprehension)

Which of the following is FALSE about student loans?

a. They are always available to students, no matter what the student's status is.
b. They are a legitimate way to pay for your college education.
c. They can determine whether you go to college or not.
d. They can damage your credit permanently if managed poorly.

Reading Comprehension Question 9.4 (Analysis)

The main reason why there is a chapter on trying to maintain balance in your life while in college is

a. because most students are not able to manage themselves in college
b. because most students are unaware that it is important to maintain balance in their lives during their college careers
c. because most students do not realize that maintaining balance will ensure that they have all the money they need and enable them to get high grades in college
d. because most parents never teach college students about how to avoid stress in college

Summary

In this chapter you learned some important principles about trying to maintain balance in your life during college. Four kinds of balance are physical, psychological, academic, and financial balance. Some tips on how to maintain balance in these four areas were discussed and websites were provided for the student to explore additional information about these areas. Maintaining a successful balance in your life is, indeed, a key to student success.

REVIEW QUESTIONS 9.1

Instructions: Following are five true-false statements taken from the information in this chapter. First, try to answer them without looking back at the chapter. Then review the chapter to see how well you did.

Question & Answer	Rationale
Circle true or false for each of the following statements.	**Write an explanation stating why each statement is true or false.**
1. Being "in balance" means that you do not have any illnesses. **True or False**	Your Rationale:
2. Stress is a normal part of the college experience. **True or False**	Your Rationale:
3. It is best to remain in your room when you are feeling stressed in college so you do not disturb other students. **True or False**	Your Rationale:
4. When you hear your roommate talking about suicide or how troubled she is, the best thing you can do is avoid the issue because it will make her feel even more depressed if you talk with her about it. **True or False**	Your Rationale:
5. Financial balance means that you are able to take out loans to pay for your entire college education as well as your living expenses during college. **True or False**	Your Rationale:

Name: ______________________

Chapter Nine **Study Guide**

Chapter 9, Goal 1: Define balance and list four important elements of balance in your life at college.

Questions	Answers & Notes

Name: ____________________________

Chapter Nine

Study Guide

Chapter 9, Goal 2: Describe the characteristics of a college student who maintains balance in his or her life during college.

Questions	Answers & Notes

Name: ______________________________

Chapter Nine | **Study Guide**

Chapter 9, Goal 3: Discuss at least five ways to maintain academic balance in your first year of college.

Questions	Answers & Notes

Name: ______________________________

Chapter Nine

Study Guide

Chapter 9, Goal 4: Discuss at least five ways to maintain psychological balance in your first year of college.

Questions	Answers & Notes

Name: ____________________

Chapter Nine **Study Guide**

Chapter 9, Goal 5: Discuss at least five ways to maintain physical balance in your first year of college.

Questions	Answers & Notes

Name: ____________________

Chapter Nine **Study Guide**

Chapter 9, Goal 6: Discuss at least five ways to maintain financial balance in your first year of college.

Questions	Answers & Notes

Name: ______________________________

Preparing for Class:
Use This Page to Record Questions or Insights to Discuss in Class.

ASSIGNMENT 9.1

Maintaining Balance in Life During College

Goal:

The purpose of this activity is for the student to understand the concept of maintaining balance in life while taking college courses and to have a plan in place for doing so.

Objective:

The student will work toward an overall plan for maintaining balance in four areas of life while in college.

Instructions:

Read the chapter to make sure that you understand why you should be concerned about balance in life; then follow these steps to create your plan:

Step 1: Outline the four major areas in which balance is important (academic, psychological, physical, and financial).

Step 2: Determine what activities would most suit you in trying to maintain balance in these four areas:

academic:

psychological:

physical:

financial:

Step 3: Share your plan for maintaining balance with a friend or mentor to get ideas for improvement or changes to your plan.

Step 4: Evaluate whether or not your plan is working by assessing how you are behaving and feeling during your first semester of college.

Step 5: If you find you are not in balance in some aspect of your life, seek help to get assistance in recovering your balance and maintaining it.

Chapter 10 Roadmap

Planning for the Future: What Courses Should I Take?

In this chapter you will learn about the typical requirements for graduation from college, including core curriculum requirements and the requirements of a particular major. We will discuss some practical information about selecting courses and planning when to take them. For a follow-up assignment you will use the information in this chapter along with information from your college to plan which courses you will take next semester and also to design your long-term graduation plan.

This chapter roadmap page presents the formal learning goals for this chapter and a checklist that you should follow as you read and study the chapter.

Student Learning Goals for This Chapter

After completing this chapter the student should be able to do the following:

1. Understand the basic requirements for graduation from college in general.
2. Select a major and identify which courses are required for graduation within the chosen major area of study.
3. Calculate a grade point average when given the appropriate variables.
4. Design a long-term graduation plan that includes a list of all of the courses needed to graduate.
5. Prepare a semester registration plan based on a long-term graduation plan.

Checklist for This Chapter

Target date/ deadline	Check when completed	Activity
________	❑	1. Complete Critical Thinking Activity 10.1.
________	❑	2. Convert the learning goals above to questions that you can answer as you read the chapter. Write your questions on the study guide pages near the end of this chapter.
________	❑	3. Read the chapter.
________	❑	4. Try to answer the reading comprehension questions as you come to them in the chapter. Check each answer by comparing it to the list of correct answers in the back of the book. If any answer was not correct, then review the passages preceding the question to see why you missed the question.
________	❑	5. Use the study guide pages near the end of this chapter to answer the questions you created in Step 2. Once completed, these pages will be your study guide.
________	❑	6. Write down any questions, insights, or comments that you have as you read so that you can bring them up in class (if applicable).
________	❑	7. Complete Review Questions 10.1.
________	❑	8. Complete Assignment 10.1 (Long-Term Graduation Plan).
________	❑	9. Complete Assignment 10.2 (Semester Registration Plan).
________	❑	10. Visit your advisor for registration (if applicable).

CRITICAL THINKING ACTIVITY 10.1

Consider the following questions related to planning for your graduation from college. Put a check mark in the appropriate column, depending on whether or not you know the information necessary to answer the question. Check the YES column if you are very confident that you know the information. Check the NO column if you don't know the information—or if you think you know, but are not completely confident.

INFORMATION OF IMPORTANCE	YES (Confident)	NO (Not Sure)
1. What are the courses that you are required to take for your major area of study?		
2. How many credit hours are required to graduate?		
3. How many credit hours should you take each semester? Why?		
4. How do you calculate your GPA?		
5. How does your GPA affect your graduation?		
6. Should you take an online course?		
7. Exactly when and where should you submit your application for graduation?		

ANALYSIS		
A. How many checks are in the YES column?	+	
B. How many checks are in the NO column?		–
C. Subtract the number of NO checks from the number of YES checks. This is your score for this exercise.		

REFLECTION
If your score for this exercise is less than 4, then your lack of knowledge about these issues puts you in greater danger of not graduating. The good news is that this chapter provides the answers for all of these questions.

Planning for the Future:
What Courses Should I Take?

10

> *It is as difficult to achieve a goal that you don't have as it is to come back from a place that you have never been.*
>
> — *Zig Ziglar*[1]

Why are you attending college? Some students start out at a two-year college and plan to graduate with an associate degree and then transfer to a four-year college or university. Other students who start at a two-year college plan to earn thirty or more hours of college-level credit and then transfer to another institution to obtain their final degree. These are two of the most common goals that two-year college students work toward.

Most students who go straight to a four-year college plan to graduate from that same college, earning a bachelor's degree. It is becoming more and more common for students who complete a bachelor's degree to continue their education by pursuing a master's degree or a doctorate (PhD). You may elect to pursue an advanced degree (a master's, PhD, or a professional degree—such as a medical or law degree) at the same university where you got your bachelor's if they have the program you need, but it is more likely that you will move to a new institution. If you continue beyond the master's degree level to a doctorate, then you may transfer to yet a different university. There are also many programs that allow you to pursue a PhD directly after finishing your bachelor's, without obtaining a master's first. After obtaining a PhD, many graduate students go on to pursue postdoctoral research—almost always at a new institution. The question is "How do you get there from here?" This chapter is designed to answer that question by helping you to plan for graduation at the bachelor's-degree level.

One of the most important things you have learned from reading this book is that planning is a major key to success. To design your long-term graduation plan, you will need to understand both the core curriculum requirements (courses required for all majors) and the requirements for your chosen field of study. This chapter will describe, in some detail, the core curriculum and other requirements for graduation. We will include some practical information about how courses and credit work in college, how to calculate your grade point average (GPA), how to decide which courses to take, and how many courses to take each term. You will be able to use the information in this chapter along with information from your college (usually found in the college catalog) to design your long-term graduation plan.

Reading Comprehension Question 10.1 (Knowledge)

To design your long-term graduation plan, you will need to do which of the following?

a. Understand the core curriculum requirements as well as the requirements for your chosen field of study

b. Know all the courses that are offered in your college system

c. Use a software program called "Plan It" on your college's website

d. None of the above

10.1 Graduation Requirements

Many students begin college with only a vague idea about how to proceed past the first semester. You may realize that you are here to take a lot of classes and then graduate. That is a good start. However, sometime during your first semester you need to pay attention to the specifics of what you are going to do each semester between now and graduation.

Most likely when you were a high school freshman, you didn't have to worry too much about exactly what you would do and which courses you would take as a sophomore, junior, and senior. With the exception of a few choices, the school probably took care of most of that for you. Colleges also help you a little by setting up programs of study for specific majors and publishing those in the college catalog. However, in college you have many more choices, and it is mostly up to you to create and follow through with a program that will result in your desired outcome.

Let's explore some background information that you need to know before you create your own graduation plan. What courses do you have to take? When, and in what order, should you take them? How many of them should you take at once? Which courses should you avoid? How can you monitor your progress as you take courses?

The Core Curriculum

In most colleges, there are certain courses that everyone must take, regardless of your major area of study. These courses are often referred to as **the core curriculum**. These usually include some introductory courses from a variety of disciplines that are designed to help you become a well-rounded liberal arts graduate. Everyone with a college degree, regardless of the major, is expected to have some command of the humanities, the field of mathematics, the natural sciences, and the social sciences. In the United States, the federal government mandates a basic knowledge of U.S. history and government, so you can expect to take some required courses related to those topics as well. Most of the core courses are completed during the first two years of college. This makes planning during the first two years a little easier since all students will have to take courses from these categories regardless of major.

Core requirements may vary somewhat from college to college, but there is a general consistency that makes transferring easier. Many students begin their college experience at a two-year college where they complete their core requirements, and then transfer to a four-year college or university to complete the second half of their baccalaureate, or bachelor's, degree.

You will enjoy courses related to your chosen major during the second two years of a four-year program. Some private colleges may have a core regimen that looks different, at least in terms of the course titles, from the core curriculum found in their public counterparts. However, the courses usually still offer a foundation in the same variety of disciplines. If this is the case at your college, it is critical that you work with your advisor in order to develop an enrollment plan that will ensure your successful completion of college in an appropriate time frame.

The College Catalog

It is wise to consult the college catalog during your first semester and use it to create a list of the courses you plan to take from the first semester until graduation. Of course, this plan can be adjusted along the way as new courses become available. You should check course offerings every term to see if a new class is available that fulfills one of your existing requirements. Course offerings will also vary more for some majors than others. The college catalog usually provides a list of the core curriculum and the additional courses that are required for graduation in each major. This information is typically organized by department and then by specific majors. A large university may organize the catalog by college, then department, and finally by major. By definition (in the United States), a university is a collection of colleges (for example, the College of Arts and Sciences, the College of Education, the College of Nursing, and so on).

If your college catalog does not list the information you need, then be sure to learn where to find the course descriptions and the list of courses in the core curriculum that are required for graduation at your specific college. Many colleges have abandoned the paper hard copy of the catalog and provide, instead, a catalog in electronic format online.

It would be beneficial if you can talk with your advisor to determine whether your college has a "Core Curriculum Worksheet" or a "Graduation Planning Worksheet" for specific majors, which you can use to determine your own graduation requirements. If so, use that worksheet to plan your progress through college. If not, you can create your own by using your college catalog and the generic worksheet in Assignment 10.1 at the end of this chapter.

Courses and Credit

College courses are measured in units called **credit hours**. In most colleges, the number of credit hours assigned to a course is usually correlated with the number of minutes per week that the class meets. Usually, a fifty-minute class session corresponds to one credit hour. For example, an English composition course that meets fifty minutes, three times a week would be a three-credit hour course. Exceptions to this pattern include courses with labs, or something like a physical education course that meets twice a week but earns only one credit hour. Once you determine which courses you need to take and understand the credit hour scheme at your own college, you will be ready to plan your course load for each semester.

Your **academic program** is the series of courses that are required in order to earn your college degree. Exactly which courses are included in the list differs, depending on your major area of study (sometimes called your program of study). You need to create a **long-term graduation plan** in order to ensure that you take the courses that are required for your major area of study.

Courses to Avoid

There are so many choices in college. It seems like there are courses on every topic imaginable. Sometimes, even though I already hold advanced degrees, I look at the course list and ponder how much I would enjoy taking some of the classes I see. For example, I think I would enjoy taking a foreign language just to broaden my horizons—and that I would enjoy taking a studio art class such as pottery or watercolor just to scratch my creative itch. I suppose I could take those courses, if I have the time and am willing to pay for them.

As a new college freshman, you may be attracted to many of the courses that you see listed in the catalog; however, you are not truly free to take just any course. You have to take the courses that are listed as required for your particular major. Some majors allow a limited number of elective courses—but even then, you must choose your elective from a list of elective courses that are approved for that major. If you are an art major, then you could probably use a pottery course for your major. It may even be a required course for an art major. But if you are a business major, then it is unlikely that you will be allowed to use a pottery course on your graduation application. When considering any course, you must ask yourself, "*Does this course fit in my graduation plan?*"

Does this mean that the college won't allow you to take a studio art course if you are a business major? No, it does not. Most likely, if you are admitted as a student in good standing, the college will let you take any course (as long as you pay the tuition). Thus, a business major could take a pottery course merely for personal growth, but the credits earned for the pottery course would not be considered as credit toward graduation for a business major. Certainly, you can take extra courses if you like—as long as you understand that they are extra and that you still have to earn all of the credits you need for graduation using other approved courses. Too many extra courses and not enough required courses could mean that you have to attend college longer than you had planned before you graduate.

There is one more thing that you should know about extra courses. Remember that all of the courses that you take, whether required or extra, will be used to calculate your cumulative grade point average. Only courses actually listed on your graduation application will be used to calculate your graduation GPA, but all courses are used for the cumulative GPA. In addition, when you transfer to another institution, the college will forward all of your grades to the receiving institution, not just those that you used for your degree. Additional information about this appears later in this chapter under the heading "How to Calculate Your GPA."

If you are interested in an extra course but you do not want to receive a grade for it on your transcript, then you can **audit** the course. When you audit, you still pay tuition; you get to participate in the course fully, but you do not receive a grade for the course. A student once told me that he audited a golf course (physical education) every semester in college because he loved to play golf. He didn't need those physical education credits, but as a student on a tight budget he reasoned that tuition was less expensive than green fees. The local country club had an arrangement with the college such that students in the golf class would be exempt from green fees for the duration of the course.

Online Courses

Online courses are becoming ubiquitous in colleges around the county. Many colleges even offer entire degree programs online. Who should take an online course? The answer to this question varies. Your level of experience, level of comfort, and level of maturity influence your likelihood of success in an online class.

During your college experience you are likely to experience one or more of three types of online course work: 1) the online course, a course that is taught entirely online; 2) the hybrid course, a course that is taught partially online and partially in a classroom; and 3) the online supported course, a course that is taught face-to-face in a classroom but that includes handouts, study guides, or other support tools for students that are provided online.

Following are six things that you should know about online classes:

1. Online classes may be more convenient than face-to-face (F2F) classes; however, they require just as much time, if not more, than would the same course in a F2F format.
2. Online courses often have strict deadlines throughout the semester. Just because it is online does not mean that the students can submit assignments for a grade anytime they wish before the end of the semester.
3. Online courses often require more writing than would the same course in a F2F format.
4. Online courses require that the student is mature and disciplined enough to work independently in order to be successful.
5. Online courses require that the student has an Internet connection at home or otherwise has unlimited access to a computer and the Internet.
6. Online courses require that the student knows how to use the computer and the Internet. This usually involves, but is not limited to, using email, attaching files, using word processing software, reading and writing in a discussion board, taking timed quizzes, uploading, downloading, and performing simple operating system functions like copy, cut, and paste.

Want to learn more?

Try this resource.

Here is an online questionnaire that will help you decide if online courses are right for you:

The Smarter Measures Tool
http://bvtlab.com/hw79p

Planning Your Semester Course Load

How many credit hours should you take each semester? The answer to this question varies, based on the needs of each student.

Different colleges may have different credit hour requirements. You will need to determine what the specific requirements are at your college. To illustrate the process in this book, we will use the typical semester system scheme.

In the typical semester program, a course load of about 16 credit hours per semester is considered normal. To be considered a full-time student (which is often necessary for financial aid purposes), you must typically be enrolled in 12 credit hours. The difference is because the federal government, rather than the college, determines the definition of *full-time* for federal financial aid. Thus, 12 credit hours are required if you are to be considered a full-time student for financial aid (grants or loans), but 16 credit hours is considered "normal" because you would have to take an average of 16 credit hours per semester to graduate with a four-year degree within four years.

Attending less than full time does not prevent a student from receiving financial aid, but it may affect the amount of aid received at one time. Some students also need to take at least 12 credit hours to satisfy the requirements of scholarships, to receive discounts on auto insurance or to remain as dependents on their parents' health insurance policy, to be allowed to live in a dorm on campus, or to be allowed to play for a campus sports team.

Most colleges also specify a maximum number of credit hours (usually 17 or 18) in which the student can enroll without special permission. You should check your college's policy if you are interested in taking more than the maximum number of credits in one semester. Usually, an academic official, such as the dean or the vice president for academic affairs, must grant the permission. You should not enroll in more credit hours than you are able to keep up with and still earn high grades.

In the typical semester system program, students are required to earn about 60 credit hours to graduate with a two-year diploma and about 120 credit hours to graduate with a four-year diploma. In this case, the normal course load for a semester is 15 credit hours. The reason is simple: four semesters at 15 hours each adds up to the 60 hours required for the two-year degree, and eight semesters at 15 hours each adds up to the 120 hours required for the four-year degree.

Many colleges require a few extra courses in the core curriculum beyond the credit hours required for a degree. These are courses that the institution feels are necessary for a well-rounded education and may be only 1 or 2 credit hours each. Examples of such courses may be health, first aid, and physical education courses. If your college requires an additional 4 credit hours total for these types of courses—such that the total number of credit hours required for the first two years was 64 hours—then the normal course load would be 16 credit hours for each semester. Table 10.1 illustrates this scenario.

Table 10.1 Credit Hour Scenario for the First Two Years Without Summer Courses

	Fall Semester	Spring Semester	Summer Semester	Total Hours
Year One	16 hours	16 hours	Zero hours	= 64 hours
Year Two	16 hours	16 hours	Zero hours	

Alternatively, you could complete the 64 hours within two years by taking 12 hours each fall, 12 hours each spring, and 8 hours each summer as is illustrated in Table 10.2.

Table 10.2 Credit Hour Scenario for the First Two Years with Summer Courses

	Fall Semester	Spring Semester	Summer Semester	Total Hours
Year One	12 hours	12 hours	8 hours	= 64 hours
Year Two	12 hours	12 hours	8 hours	

If you wish to complete these requirements within two years and you do not plan to take any summer courses, then you would need to take 16 credit hours each semester, or you would have to plan to attend an additional semester to earn enough credits before you graduate.

Don't be discouraged if you do not graduate within two years for an associate's degree or within four years for a bachelor's degree. *Very few people do.* According to the U.S. Census, the average number of years that it took students to complete a bachelor's degree in 2004 was 6.5 years, and the average number of years it took to complete an associate's degree was 4.4 years.[2] What matters most is that you do, in fact, finish the program of study and graduate. Those students who have many time-consuming, non-academic responsibilities (work, children, etc.) may choose to enroll in less than a normal load in order to maintain good grades while juggling those additional responsibilities. You must also keep your grade point average high in order to graduate. Take as many courses as you can responsibly handle. You must devote enough time to the course to learn the material and to be able to demonstrate what you have learned.

When you are planning which courses to take, keep in mind that it is not a good practice to take all easy classes (or classes that are easy for you) in one semester because that means that in the future you will likely have a semester with all difficult classes. Instead, select a balance of courses with some that you will find easy and some that you will find challenging.

A balanced schedule will make it easier for you to maintain the required GPA necessary for graduation. Since you must maintain a certain grade point average (GPA) in order to graduate, you need to know how to calculate your GPA.

How to Calculate Your GPA

The section of the chapter about how to calculate your GPA is included because your GPA sometimes affects which courses you select for a particular semester. The GPA is calculated as the number of grade points earned divided by the number of credit hours attempted.

Suppose that a student took five classes that added up to 12 credit hours. How would you calculate the GPA for those courses? First, you would need to determine how many grade points the student has earned. The number of points earned for each credit hour is as follows:

A = 4 grade points,

B = 3 grade points,

C = 2 grade points,

D = 1 grade point, and

F = 0 grade points.

Second, multiply each class's credit hours by the grade points earned according to each letter grade to determine the grade points earned for each class. (In the example below, for the health class, 2 credit hours X 4 grade points [for an A] = 8.) Third, determine the sum of credit hours attempted. Finally, divide the sum of the grade points earned by the sum of credit hours attempted to find the grade point average.

For example, suppose Charlie Brown earned the grades specified for the following complement of courses. His GPA would be 2.5 because the total grade points (30) divided by the total number of credit hours attempted (12) equals 2.5.

Course	Credit Hours	Grade Earned	Grade Points Earned
Composition I	3	C	6
Algebra	3	C	6
Sociology	3	C	6
Health	2	A	8
Student Success	1	A	4
TOTALS	12	—	30

Many colleges calculate two types of GPA: the graduation GPA and the cumulative GPA. Only courses that count toward graduation are used to calculate the graduation GPA. Those are the courses that the student needs to graduate and that are listed on the graduation application. However, all of the courses that a student has taken are used when calculating the *cumulative* GPA. If a student has taken the same course twice, both grades will be used to calculate the cumulative GPA. It is the cumulative GPA that is usually transferred to other colleges since all of the courses on your transcript are sent to the receiving institution. Check your college catalog to see if this is the rule at your college. There may be some variation of policy from college to college.

Reading Comprehension Question 10.3 (Inferential Comprehension)

Why would you need to know how to calculate your GPA?

a. Because sometimes your GPA will determine which courses you might need to take in a given semester

b. Because doing math is important for college students

c. Because your GPA might determine what type of job you can obtain after graduation

d. All of the above

Graduation Application

The *graduation application* has already been mentioned in this chapter, but it deserves additional attention. It is not the case that you just go along from year to year taking courses until one day the college calls you and says, "You are graduating this semester, so remember to show up for the ceremony ... and wear a robe." Instead, graduation is an event that is planned well in advance and usually involves the completion of some paperwork by the student. Some colleges call the paperwork "the graduation application," and there is usually a small fee for submitting the application.

What is on the application? It usually asks for your name, student ID, address, major, name of your advisor, and also includes a checklist of the courses required for your major, along with a space to indicate the grade earned in that course and the date that the course was taken. The graduation application form may have a place for you to list your name *as you want it to appear* on your diploma, so be careful about how you fill it out. If you write a nickname like "Butch" on the form, you might be very disappointed at graduation to receive a diploma with Butch Williams engraved on it, rather than David Alexander Williams, Jr. as you expected.

A graduation application form can usually be downloaded from your registrar's web page. In most colleges, you must submit a completed graduation application to the registrar by a *deadline during the semester prior to your last semester of classes*. Check your college's official calendar (usually online) to determine the deadline, or call the registrar's office.

For example, suppose you were planning to graduate after the end of the spring semester of 2020. In that case, you probably need to submit your graduation application before the deadline during the middle of the fall semester of 2019. The graduation application usually requires several signatures—your signature as well as those of some other academic officials (such as your academic advisor and possibly the chair for the department or division of your academic major). Therefore, when the appropriate semester comes, make an appointment with your advisor early in the semester so that he or she can help you get the form signed and submitted on time.

You need to start thinking about that graduation application from your very first semester in college. You need to plan ahead as much as you can for which courses you will take and in what order. In other words, you need a long-term graduation plan.

Reading Comprehension Question 10.2 (Literal Comprehension)

The book that you are reading now tells you about which of the following?

a. About the requirements for graduation at your college
b. About all of your institutional requirements
c. About how to develop a long-term plan for graduation
d. All of the above

10.2 Designing Your Long-Term Graduation Plan

Now that you know some of the basic information about course credits, course loads, and GPA requirements, you are ready to design your long-term graduation plan.

The long-term graduation plan is really very simple. It is **a list of all of the courses that you plan to take, arranged in the order that you plan to take them**. You can use the form provided in Assignment 10.1 to create your own plan. The form provides a series of boxes, representing each semester from your first semester until the term you plan to graduate. You should label each box with the date of the semester and list titles of the courses that you plan to take that semester in the box.

In order to design the plan, you will need to decide a few things:

- Which courses are required for your program of study (major)?
- Which of the courses you plan to take have prerequisites? (courses you must complete prior to enrolling)
- How many credit hours would you like to take each semester?
- Would you like to take classes in the summer?

Step 1: Select an academic major

You should select an academic major as soon as possible because it will help you to be more effective in your planning. Experts who study issues related to higher education—such as Stan Jones, the founder of Complete College America—have suggested that the students who are most likely to be successful in college are those who choose a program and stick with it.

One benefit of working toward a particular major is that you will know exactly which courses you need to take. As previously stated, a list of courses associated with each major is usually found in the college catalog. There are certain courses specified in the list that are required, not optional. The required major courses usually account for only a portion of the course credits required to graduate. The additional credits will be earned by taking elective courses. Elective does not mean that you can select any course that you wish, but rather that you may select any course within a specified list of elective courses. These elective courses are also listed in the college catalog and are dependent on which major you have chosen. You may have a bit of fun browsing that list and anticipating some of those courses.

You should know that there are some (but not many) majors that allow little or no elective choice. For example, in one college where I taught, the education major had very few elective choices. This was simply because there were so many courses required by that state's accrediting agency that were considered essential for anyone who planned to teach; by the time you took them all, you had enough credits for a degree.

If you choose a major during your freshman year but later change your mind, you can change your major. Changing your major during the first two years of college is not usually problematic because most of the courses you will take during those years are core courses that can be used for any major. If you do happen to take a course that can only be used for your initial major, then you would not be able to use that course on your graduation application after switching majors.

In most colleges, when you choose a major or change your major, you will need to complete and submit some type of form (for example, a "Change of Program of Study" form) to the registrar in order to make your choice official. These forms are usually available on the web page for the registrar or in the office of the registrar.

You can still work on a graduation plan even if you have not decided which program of study you would like to pursue. Simply insert a placeholder for those courses into your long-term plan. For example, you could write, "major area course #1," "major area course #2," and so on. Plan as best you can; then when you decide on a major, you can change those placeholders to the appropriate courses. Obviously, this placeholder strategy is not the best method because it leaves you with a lot of unknowns in your long-term plan, but it is still better than having no plan at all.

If you are interested in two or three different majors and are having trouble deciding, you may also wish to complete more than one graduation plan worksheet (one for each major). Then, you can compare them side-by-side and easily identify which courses they all have in common and how they differ. First, take the courses that your favorite majors have in common. That will give you a little more time to think about which major you want to ultimately pursue.

The U.S. Census Bureau provides some data about how many Americans graduate with each type of major. There is also census data about what types of jobs people are doing who have graduated with a certain major and how much money they have been earning in that capacity. In general, the data show that the higher the education people have, the greater their earning potential. It also suggests that people with college degrees in some majors earn more than people with degrees in other majors. If you are looking for the major that has the most earning power, then you will be interested in that aspect of the data. Keep in mind, however, that earning power may not be the only criteria that you want to use when deciding your career. As a wise man once said, "*Pick a job that you enjoy doing, and you will never have to go to work.*" Another interesting observation about the data is that many people acquired jobs or careers that were not directly connected to their undergraduate college major.

Want to learn more?

Try this resource.

If you want to know more about the number of people who earned each degree, the types of jobs they do, and the amount they earn, you can visit the *American Community Survey Data on Educational Attainment, Field of Degree Infographics: 2010 - Pathways After a Bachelor's Degree* webpage:
http://bvtlab.com/7Vq57

This webpage allows you to "select a major to view" from a list (see below). Then, it displays full color charts that present the data for the major you selected. The data is from the 2010 U.S. Census about the number of people who earned each degree, the types of jobs they do, and the amount they earn (total, over the course of their careers).

- Biological, Agricultural, and Environmental Sciences
- Business
- Communications
- Computers, Mathematics, and Statistics
- Education
- Engineering
- Liberal Arts and History
- Literature and Languages
- Physical and Related Science
- Psychology
- Science and Engineering Related Fields
- Social Science
- Visual and Performing Arts

Step 2: Identify prerequisites

In order to create a graduation plan, you will need to determine if there are prerequisite requirements that are associated with any of the courses you plan to take. A **prerequisite** is a requirement that must be met before you are allowed to take the course. A common type of prerequisite is prior completion of another course.

As an example, suppose that Composition I, Composition II, and World Literature are all required for your major. Now, let's say that Composition II is a prerequisite for World Literature. Therefore, you cannot enroll in World Literature until you have first successfully completed Composition II. Composition II also has a prerequisite: Composition I. Therefore, when you are planning which humanities courses to take over several semesters, you should start with Composition I, then plan to take Composition II during the following semester, and finally plan to take a literature course during your third semester. If you wait until the semester before you graduate to take the Composition II course, then you would have to hang around an additional semester to take the remaining required literature course.

Often an introductory level course will be a prerequisite for a higher level course in the same discipline. For example, in many colleges, the Introduction to Sociology course must be taken prior to any higher-level sociology course, such as Marriage and Family or Classical Sociological Theory. This is because there is information in the introductory level course that you will need to understand before you attempt to tackle the higher level course.

The main point here is that you must *plan ahead*. By the end of your first semester in college, you should have planned what courses you will take (and when) for your entire first two years of college, at least.

Step 3: Determine when specific courses are available

Another important question to address when designing your plan is "In which semesters will my college be offering the courses that I need?" Every course is not offered every semester. Some courses are offered only in fall, whereas others are offered only in spring. In many colleges the summer schedule changes from year to year, depending on budget issues and the availability of instructors. And for some majors course offerings vary, so that each term new courses are available to fulfill the same requirement (be sure to consult your advisor about the requirements for your specific major). However, most colleges publish a list of course offerings well in advance and allow you to view the list of course offerings for future semesters via a link on your college website. Your advisor may also be able to help you discover when and with what frequency a particular course is offered.

Step 4: Record when you plan to take each required course

Follow the instructions provided with Assignment 10.1 to create a table that shows when you plan to take each of the courses that are required for your major. On the following pages you will find a partial example of a completed "Long-term Graduation Plan." There is also an explanation of the different aspects of the example.

The example in Figure 10.1 is for a student who wishes to graduate in four years and does not wish to take classes during the summer. If you were planning to take classes during the summer, then you would need to record the titles of those courses in the column for summer.

Reading Comprehension Question 10.4 (Analysis)

Why is it important for you to understand this chapter?

a. It provides information to guide you in designing your entire academic program at college.
b. It is only important for those who know their major ahead of time.
c. It is not important for all students, only those who plan to transfer to a four-year college.
d. None of the above
e. All of the above

Figure 10.1 Partial Example of a Graduation Plan Worksheet

❶ FALL (Year: 2016)	❶ SPRING (Year: 2017)	❶ SUMMER (2017)
❷ English Composition I (3 hrs.)	❷ English Composition II (3 hrs.)	
❷❹ Pre-calculus (3 hrs.)	❷❹ Calculus I (3 hrs.)	
U.S. History (3 hrs.)	U.S. Government (3 hrs.)	
Public Speaking (3 hrs.)	Social science elective: Sociology (3 hrs.)	
College Success (3 hrs.)	Other required course (3 hrs.)	
Fitness Walking (1 hr.)	Other PE course (1 hr.)	
TOTAL HRS. = 16	TOTAL HRS. = 16	

❶ FALL (Year: 2017)	❶ SPRING (Year: 2018)	❶ SUMMER (2018)
❷ World Literature (3 hrs.)	Humanities elective: Intro to Art (3 hrs.)	
❷❸❹ First required science (4 hrs.)	❷ Second required science (4 hrs.)	
Social science elective: Psychology (3 hrs.)	Other required course (3 hrs.)	
Other required course (3 hrs.)	Other required course (3 hrs.)	
Other required course (3 hrs.)	Other required course (3 hrs.)	
TOTAL HRS. = 16	TOTAL HRS. = 16	

❶ FALL (Year: 2018)	❶ SPRING (Year: 2019)	❶ SUMMER (2019)

❶ FALL (Year: 2019)	❶ SPRING (Year: 2020)
Note: Submit graduation application.	Graduate!

Examine the plan. Is a strategy apparent? Note the following characteristics of the example worksheet (these descriptions match the number labels on the example figure):

❶ Record the appropriate dates for each semester in the header for each box.

❷ Note how this student planned courses with prerequisites in order—thus, the prerequisites will be taken prior to the courses that require them for the humanities sequence, the mathematics sequence, and the science sequence.

❸ This student used a placeholder, "First required science," because she has not yet decided which science course she prefers. Since some science courses must be taken in sequence (i.e., Biology I before Biology II), she has planned accordingly.

❹ Note that this student has planned to take the required mathematics courses in the first year and then the required science course in the second year. This is because the student is aware that having a stronger mathematics background before you take science may help you perform better in the science class. (Some science courses may have a math course as a prerequisite.)

Summary

In this chapter you learned about the value of a long-term graduation plan and how to design such a plan. In order to design an effective plan, you need to understand the core curriculum requirements, requirements for the major you wish to pursue, how to determine an appropriate semester course load, and how to determine if online courses are appropriate for you, as well as how to calculate your GPA.

The things you learned in this chapter will enable you to create a long-term academic plan that lists all of the courses you are required to take in college in the order in which you plan to take them. Once you have done this, you will be prepared to plan your schedule for next semester. These tasks will be easier if you have selected a major because you will know exactly what courses you need to include in your plan. Take time to create your long-term academic plan and to complete your semester registration planning form *before* you visit your advisor. Take the completed forms with you when you visit your advisor so that you can talk with your advisor about them. Visit your advisor as soon as possible (you will have to make an appointment) when registration starts. In most colleges, the most popular courses and courses offered at the time of day most preferred by students tend to fill up quickly. If you wait too late to register, then you may find that your first choices have filled up and are closed.

The student will benefit most from this chapter if he or she does the following:

1. Selects a major (program of study)
2. Creates a written long-term graduation plan
3. Completes a semester registration planning form based on the information in the long-term plan
4. Makes an appointment with his or her academic advisor as soon as possible *before* registration and registers for the courses specified in the long-term plan
5. Saves the "Core Curriculum Worksheet" template that is provided in this chapter and uses it every semester to keep a record of the courses that he or she has completed with passing grades
6. Calculates his or her GPA after each semester and considers the implications for planning future courses
7. Completes and submits a graduation application form to the registrar's office on time

Review Questions

10.1

Instructions: Following are five true-false statements taken from the information in this chapter. First, try to answer them without looking back at the chapter. Then review the chapter to see how well you did.

Question & Answer	Rationale
Circle True or False for each of the following.	**Write an explanation for why it is true or false.**
1. If a student plans to graduate with an Associate Degree (from a college that uses the semester system) within two years without taking summer courses, then he or she will have to take 16 or 17 credit hours of courses each semester. **True or False**	Your Rationale:
2. You don't really need to know how to calculate your GPA because there is no reason to know what your GPA is until you are ready to graduate. **True or False**	Your Rationale:
3. It does not matter which semester you plan to take a specific course because all of the courses are always offered in both Fall and Spring semester. **True or False**	Your Rationale:
4. According to experts, students are more likely to be successful if they pick a program and stick with it. **True or False**	Your Rationale:
5. A long-term academic plan will lead you to successful completion of your academic program. **True or False**	Your Rationale:

Name: ______________________________

Chapter Ten | Study Guide

Chapter 10, Goal 1: Understand the basic requirements for graduation from college in general.

Questions	Answers & Notes

Name: ____________________

Chapter Ten **Study Guide**

Chapter 10, Goal 2: Select a major, and identify which courses are required for graduation within the chosen major area of study.

Questions	Answers & Notes

Name: ______________________________

Chapter Ten

Study Guide

Chapter 10, Goal 3: Calculate a grade point average when given the appropriate variables.

Questions	Answers & Notes

Name: ______________________________

Chapter Ten

Study Guide

Chapter 10, Goal 4: Design a long-term graduation plan that includes a list of all of the courses needed to graduate.

Questions	Answers & Notes

Name: ____________________

Chapter Ten **Study Guide**

Chapter 10, Goal 5: Prepare a semester registration plan based on a long-term graduation plan.

Questions	Answers & Notes

Name: ____________________

Preparing for Class:
Use This Page to Record Questions or Insights to Discuss in Class.

Assignment 10.1

Design Your Long-Term Graduation Plan

Goal:

The purpose of this activity is for the student to understand the course requirements for a particular program of study and to create a long-term graduation plan.

Objective:

The student will construct a long-term graduation plan.

Instructions:

Read the chapter to make sure that you understand why you should create your long-term graduation plan and then follow these steps:

Step 1: Select a major program of study.

Step 2: Determine what courses are required for graduation under your program of study.

Step 3: Determine when (which semesters) the courses are offered and whether any of them have prerequisites.

Step 4: Write the titles of the courses that you plan take in the space provided on the *Long-term Graduation Plan* worksheet provided on the next page.

Step 5: Show your plan to your academic advisor when you visit him or her for registration. Ask your advisor to confirm that your plan is sound.

Long-Term Graduation Plan Worksheet

FALL (Year: ________)	SPRING (Year: ________)	SUMMER (Year: _______)
TOTAL HRS. =	TOTAL HRS. =	TOTAL HRS. =

FALL (Year: ________)	SPRING (Year: ________)	SUMMER (Year: _______)
TOTAL HRS. =	TOTAL HRS. =	TOTAL HRS. =

FALL (Year: ________)	SPRING (Year: ________)	SUMMER (Year: _______)
TOTAL HRS. =	TOTAL HRS. =	TOTAL HRS. =

FALL (Year: ________)	SPRING (Year: ________)	SUMMER (Year: _______)
TOTAL HRS. =	TOTAL HRS. =	TOTAL HRS. =

Assignment 10.2

Plan Semester Registration

Goal:

The purpose of this activity is for the student to plan a schedule in time to participate in early or regular registration.

Objective:

The student will construct a schedule for his or her next semester based on his or her *Long-term Graduation Plan* for a specific program of study and take it to his or her academic advisor for early or regular registration.

Instructions:

Use information from the chapter and your *Long-term Graduation Plan* to complete the *Semester Registration Planner* form provided on the next page. Then follow these steps:

Step 1: Determine which courses you need based on your *Long-term Graduation Plan*.

Step 2: Search the course catalog at your college to find schedule information about the courses that you need.

Step 3: Complete the *Semester Registration Planner* form.

Step 4: Make an appointment with your advisor for early or regular registration. Take your completed *Long-term Graduation Plan* worksheet and your completed *Semester Registration Planner* form to your advisor for approval and registration.

Semester Registration Planner

Take the following steps in preparation to meet with your advisor:

1. Log onto your college website and view the course schedule for next semester.
2. Observe which courses are offered and at what times they are offered.
3. Make sure that you meet the prerequisite requirements before taking the course.
4. Use the table below to record your first and second choices for courses. Be sure to include the computer code (usually a number) for the course if necessary.
5. Take this completed form with you and show it to your advisor when you meet.

Name: ______________________ **Student ID:** ______________

Major: ______________________ **Advisor:** ______________

FIRST CHOICES			
Course	**Computer Code**	**Meeting Days & Time**	**Credit Hours**
TOTAL CREDIT HOURS:			

SECOND CHOICES			
Course	**Computer Code**	**Meeting Days & Time**	**Credit Hours**
TOTAL CREDIT HOURS:			

Answer Key for Reading Comprehension Questions

Background

The reading comprehension questions found throughout this textbook have been designed to assess the following four major aspects of reading: 1) vocabulary, 2) literal comprehension, 3) inferential comprehension, and 4) analysis.

Following are descriptions for each category:

Vocabulary entails identifying the meanings of words as they are used in passages. The student may use context clues, structural analysis, and/or a general understanding of the meaning of the passage to determine the meaning of a word.

Literal Comprehension entails recognizing information and ideas presented explicitly within the passages. Literal comprehension questions require a student to recognize one or more of the following: 1) the important details or facts, 2) a sequence of events, 3) a comparative relationship, 4) a cause-and-effect relationship, or 5) the referent for which a word or group of words has been substituted in a passage.

Inferential Comprehension entails synthesizing and interpreting material that is presented in a passage. Inferential comprehension items involve the following skills: 1) identifying the main idea of a passage or paragraph, 2) inductive reasoning, 3) deductive reasoning, and 4) interpretation of figurative or other language.

Analysis is concerned with how or why a passage is written, rather than what a passage is about. In general, analysis items require inferences to be made about the style, purpose, or organization of a passage.

Follow-Up Analysis

If you score your responses to the reading questions and then tabulate how many questions you answered correctly for each of the four categories, you can gain some insight into which categories you need to work on in your reading. Use the following answer key to score your responses and then use the score analysis table to tabulate the number of correct answers for each category. There were ten questions of each type. The higher your total, the stronger your reading skill is for that category. By comparing your scores for the different types of questions, you can identify areas of strength or weakness in your reading. If you work on overcoming your weaknesses, you will be able to read and learn more effectively. When you read and learn more effectively, you will naturally earn higher grades.

Answer Key for Reading Comprehension Questions

Q #	Type	Answer	Score	Q #	Type	Answer	Score
1.1	knowledge	d		6.1	knowledge	a	
1.2	literal comprehension	a		6.2	literal comprehension	a	
1.3	inferential comprehension	a		6.3	inferential comprehension	a	
1.4	analysis	d		6.4	analysis	b	
2.1	knowledge	b		7.1	knowledge	c	
2.2	literal comprehension	e		7.2	literal comprehension	c	
2.3	inferential comprehension	a		7.3	inferential comprehension	c	
2.4	analysis	a		7.4	analysis	b	
3.1	knowledge	d		8.1	knowledge	c	
3.2	literal comprehension	e		8.2	literal comprehension	a	
3.3	inferential comprehension	d		8.3	inferential comprehension	a	
3.4	analysis	b		8.4	analysis	c	
4.1	knowledge	c		9.1	knowledge	e	
4.2	literal comprehension	c		9.2	literal comprehension	a	
4.3	inferential comprehension	d		9.3	inferential comprehension	b	
4.4	analysis	e		9.4	analysis	b	
5.1	knowledge	a		10.1	knowledge	a	
5.2	literal comprehension	b		10.2	literal comprehension	c	
5.3	inferential comprehension	a		10.3	inferential comprehension	a	
5.4	analysis	a		10.4	analysis	a	

Score Analysis Table

Category	Number Correct	Strength or Weakness?
Knowledge (Vocabulary)		
Literal Comprehension		
Inferential Comprehension		
Analysis		

Chapter One *Adjusting*

1. Churchill, W. *Searchquotes.* Retrieved February 20, 2014, from http://www.searchquotes.com/search/Some+people+ dream+of+success+while+others+wake+up+and+work+hard+at+it./

2. Rockler-Gladen, N. (2007). *High school versus college life: A freshman year guide to different student academic expectations.* Retrieved May 17, 2009, from http://collegeuniversity.suite101.com/article.cfm/high_school_versus_college

3. Altshuler Learning Enhancement Center. (2003). *How is college different from high school?* Southern Methodist University, Dallas, Texas, Altshuler Learning Enhancement Center Web site: http://smu.edu/alec/transition.asp

Chapter 2 *Organizing*

1. Carter, C., Bishop, J., & Kravits, S. L. (2006). Values, goals, time, and stress: Managing yourself. In *Keys to success: Building successful intelligence for college, career, and life* (pp. 28–52). Upper Saddle River, New Jersey: Pearson Prentice Hall.

2. MacKay, H. (2006). *Harvey MacKay quotes.* Retrieved May 17, 2009, from http://thinkexist.com/quotation/time-is-free-but-it-s-priceless-you-can-t-own-it/366011.html

3. Nist, S. and Holschuh, J. P. (2002). Timely tips: The ABC (&D)'s of time management. *College Rules!* (pp. 71–83) Berkeley, CA: Ten Speed Press.

4. Hoffman, A. J. (2008). *What every student should know about procrastination.* USA: Pearson Prentice Hall.

Chapter 3 *Listening*

1. Tucker, C. (Actor) & Ratner, B. (Director). (1998). *Rush hour.* [Motion Picture]. United States: New Line Cinema. Retrieved May 3, 2009, from http://www.entertonement.com/clips/35433/Understands-words-comin-out-of-my-mouth

2. Alighieri, D. (n.d.). *The Divine comedy.* Retrieved February 25, 2014, from http://www.quotationspage.com/quote/24494.html

3. Peterson, D. (2009). *Studying—active listening: Active listening is where studying begins.* Retrieved May 1, 2009, from http://adulted.about.com/od/intro/qt/activelistening.htm

4. Fodor, J. (n.d.). *Suggestions for active listening.* Retrieved February 25, 2004, from http://www.studygs.net/listening.htm

   Active Teaching Strategies and Learning Activities (n.d.), Retrieved February 25, 2014, from http://samples.jbpub.com/9780763749453/49451_CH09_FINAL.pdf

   Nichols, R. G. (1960). What can be done about listening. *The Supervisor's Notebook, 22*(1), 1–3.

   Stewart, P. (2007). *Listening.* Retrieved February 25, 2014, from California Polytechnic State University: San Luis Obispo, CA, Academic Skills Center (ASC), Web site: http://sas.calpoly.edu/asc/ssl/listening.html

5. Fitzgerald, F. S. (1936). *The crack-up.* Retrieved February 25, 2014, from www.quotationspage.com/quote/90.html

6. Macionis, J. (2002). *Sociology* (9th ed.) Upper Saddle River, NJ: Prentice Hall.

7. Nunn, C. (1996). Discussion in the college classroom: Triangulating observational and survey results [Electronic version]. *The Journal of Higher Education (67)*3, 243–267.

8. Leonard, E. (2008). *College success simplified* (2nd ed.). New York: Longman.

9. Leonard, E. (2007). *What every student should know about study skills.* New York: Pearson Longman.

Chapter 4 *Reading*

1. The Literacy Company. (n.d.). *Reading quotes.* Retrieved April 22, 2012, from http://www.readfaster.com/readingquotes.asp

2. Nagaraju, M. (2011). *Teaching reading to college students* [Slideshow]. Retrieved on April 22, 2012, from http://www.slideshare.net/lionnagaraju/teaching-reading-to-college-students

3. Babcock, P., & Marks, M. (2011). The falling time cost of college: Evidence from half a century of time use data. *The Review of Economics and Statistics, 93*(2), 468. Retrieved February 25, 2014, from http://ideas.repec.org/p/nbr/nberwo/15954.html

4. Boyd, D. R. (2003). *Using Textbooks Effectively: Getting Students to Read Them.* Retrieved February 24, 2014, from http://www.psychologicalscience.org/teaching/tips/tips_0603.cfm

5. Jairam, D., & Kiewra, K. A. (2009). An Investigation of the SOAR study method [Electronic version]. *Journal of Advanced Academics 20*(4), 602–629.

6. Jairam, D., & Kiewra, K. A. (2010). Helping students soar to success on computers: An investigation of the SOAR study method for computer-based learning [Electronic version]. *Journal of Educational Psychology 102*(3), 601.

7. Kiewra, K. A. (2002). How classroom teachers can help students learn and teach them how to learn [Electronic version]. *Theory Into Practice 41*(2), 71–80.

8. Kiewra, K. A. (2005). *Learn how to study and SOAR to success.* Upper Saddle River, NJ: Pearson.

9. University of Nebraska-Lincoln. (2010, August 10). College undergrads study ineffectively on computers, study finds: Students transfer bad study habits from paper to screen. *Science Daily.* Retrieved April 29, 2012, from http://www.sciencedaily.com /releases/2010/08/100810094617.htm

10. D'Agostino, S. (2011, April 8). *QED Insight.* Students don't read textbooks. Retrieved March 15, 2012, from https://qedinsight.wordpress.com/2011/04/08/students-dont-read-textbooks/

11. Academic Skills Center. (n.d.). *SQ3R Method.* Retrieved April 22, 2012, from Dartmouth College Academic Skills Center (ASC) Web site: http://www.dartmouth.edu/~acskills/docs/sq3r_method.doc

12. Robinson, Francis Pleasant. (1970). *Effective study.* New York: Harper & Row.

13. McWhorter, K. T. (2006). *Guide to college reading.* New York: Pearson.

Chapter 5 *Learning*

1. Clark, D. R. (2007). *Big dog's learning quotes.* Retrieved April 16, 2009, from http://www.skagitwatershed.org/~donclark/hrd/learnqt.html

2. Angelo, T. A. (1993). A teacher's dozen: Fourteen general, research-based principles for improving higher learning in our classrooms [Electronic version]. *AAHE Bulletin 45*(9), 3–13.

3. Brabrand, C. & Andersen, J. (Directors). (n.d.). *"Teaching teaching & understanding understanding"* [YouTube Video.]. Retrieved April 29, 2012, from http://youtu.be/w6rx GBBwVg.

4. Clark, D. R. (2007). *Learning domains or Bloom's taxonomy.* Retrieved April 18, 2009, from http://www.skagitwatershed.org/~donclark/hrd/bloom.html

5. Michaels, J., & Miethe, T. (1989). Academic effort and college grades [Electronic version]. *Social Forces 68*(1), 309–319.

6. Clark, D. R. (2007). *Memory.* Retrieved April 18, 2009, from http://www.skagitwatershed.org/~donclark/hrd/learning/memory.html

7. Shelby, H. M. (2008). Exploring cramming: Student behaviors, beliefs, and learning retention in the principles of marketing course [Electronic version]. *Journal of Marketing Education 30*(3), 226.

8. Entwistle, N. (1987). A model of the teaching-learning process. In J. T. E. Richardson, M. W. Eysenck, & D. Warren Piper (Eds.), *Student learning: Research in education and cognitive psychology.* Milton Keynes: Open University Press & SRHE.

9. Norton, L. (2009). Assessing student learning. In *Handbook for teaching and learning in higher education* (pp. 132–150.). London: Taylor & Francis Group.

10. Gibbs, G. (Ed.) (1994). *Improving student learning: Theory and practice.* Oxford: The Oxford Centre for Staff Development.

11. Tyler, R. W. (1949). *Basic principles of curriculum and instruction.* Chicago: University of Chicago Press.

12. Wiesenfeld, K. (1996). Making the grade: Many students wheedle for a degree as if it were a freebie T shirt [Electronic version]. *Newsweek 16*(16).

Chapter 6 *Styles*

1. Horner, M. (n.d.). *The Quotations page.* Retrieved March 24, 2014, from http://www.quotationspage.com/quote/3010.html

2. Felder, R. M. & Brent, R. (2005). Understanding student differences [Electronic version]. *International Journal of Engineering and Education 94*(1), 57–72.

   Felder, R. M. & Silverman, L. K. (1988). Learning and teaching styles in engineering education. [Electronic version]. *International Journal of Engineering and Education 78*(7), 674–681.

   Felder, R. M. & Soloman, B. (n.d.) Learning styles and strategies. Available at: http://www4.ncsu.edu/unity/lockers/users/f/felder/public/ILSdir/styles.htm

   Felder, R. M. & Spurlin, J. E. (2005). Applications, reliability, and validity of the index of learning styles [Electronic version]. *International Journal of Engineering Education 21*(1), 103–112.

3. Felder, R. M. & Soloman, B. (n.d.). *Learning styles and strategies.* Retrieved February 25, 2014, from http://www4.ncsu.edu/unity/lockers/users/f/felder/public/ILSdir/styles.htm

4. Felder, R. M. & Spurlin, J. E. (2005). Applications, reliability, and validity of the index of learning styles [Electronic version]. *International Journal of Engineering Education 21*(1), 103–112.

5. Felder, R. M. & Brent, R. (2005). Understanding student differences [Electronic version]. *International Journal of Engineering and Education 94*(1), 57–72.

Chapter 7 *Writing Papers*

1. King, S. (n.d.). *Goodreads.* Retrieved February 25, 2014, from http://www.goodreads.com/quotes/tag/writing?page=6

2. Rowling, J. K. (n.d.). *BrainyQuote.* Available from http://www.brainyquote.com/quotes/quotes/j/jkrowlin454020.html#MA2jKGtka40XLkjh.99

3. Caldwell Community College & Technical Institute. (2009). *Types of writing assignments you can use.* Retrieved January 21, 2013, from Caldwell Community College & Technical Institute, Hudson, NC, Web site: http://www.cccti.edu/QEP/writingtypes.htm

4. McEnerney, L. & Williams, J. (2013). *Writing in college: A short guide to college writing.* Retrieved June 1, 2013, from the University of Chicago Writing Program Web site: http://writing-program.uchicago.edu/resources/collegewriting/preparing_to_write_and_drafting.htm

Chapter 8 *Connecting*

1. Gates, B. (n.d.). *BrainyQuote.* Retrieved February 25, 2014, from www.brainyquote.com/quotes/quotes/b/billgates384628.html
2. Beecher, H. W. (n.d.). *BrainyQuote.* Retrieved May 1, 2012, from http://www.brainyquote.com/quotes/quotes/h/henrywardb383333.html
3. Foote, S. (n.d.). *Goodreads.* Retrieved February 25, 2014, from http://www.goodreads.com/quotes/126013-a-university-is-just-a-group-of-buildings-gathered-around
4. ERIAL (Ethnographic Research in Illinois Academic Libraries) project. Retrieved Jan 19, 2014, from http://www.erialproject.org/

   Asher, A., Duke, L., & Green, D. (2010, May 17). The ERIAL project: Ethnographic research in Illinois academic libraries. *Academic Commons.* Retrieved Jan 19, 2014 from http://old.academiccommons.org/commons/essay/erial-project

   Brunch, C. (2011). *Top 10 ways your college library can help you.* Retrieved Jan 19, 2014, from the Front Range Community College, CO, Writing the Front Range Blog: http://blog.frontrange.edu/2011/09/19/top-10-ways-your-college-library-can-help-you/

   Kolowich, S. (2011). Study: College students rarely use librarians' expertise. *USA Today.* Retrieved Jan 19, 2014, from http://usatoday30.usatoday.com/news/education/story/2011-08-22/Study-College-students-rarely-use-librarians-expertise/50094086/1

Chapter 9 *Balance in College Life*

1. DeGeneres, E. (n.d.). *Goodreads.* Retrieved February 25, 2014, from http://www.goodreads.com/quotes/498361
2. Chopra, D. (n.d.). *Goodreads.* Retrieved February 25. 2014, from http://www.goodreads.com/quotes/382188
3. Hinckley, G. B. (n.d.). *Goodreads.* Retrieved February 25, 2014, from http://www.goodreads.com/quotes/144912
4. Einstein, A. (n.d.). *Goodreads.* Retrieved February 25. 2014, from http://www.goodreads.com/quotes/29213
5. Olivardia, R., Pope, H. G., Jr., Mangweth, B., & Hudson, J. I. (1995). Eating disorders in college men [Electronic version]. *American Journal of Psychiatry 152*(9), 1279–85.
6. Eisenberg, D., Nicklett, E. J., Roeder, K., & Kirz, N. E. (2011). Eating disorder symptoms among college students: Prevalence, persistence, correlates, and treatment-seeking. *Journal of American College Health 59*(8), doi: 10.1080/07448481.2010.546461.
7. McCabe, M. P., Ricciardelli, L. A. (2004). A longitudinal study of pubertal timing and extreme body change behaviors among adolescent boys and girls [Electronic version]. *Adolescence* 39, 145–166.
8. McCreary, D. R., & Sadava, S. W. (2001). Gender differences in relationships among perceived attractiveness, life satisfaction, and health in adults as a function of body mass index and perceived weight [Electronic version]. *Psychology of Men and Masculinity* 2, 108–116.
9. Hudson, J. I., Hiripi, E., Pope, H. G., Jr., & Kessler, R. C. (2007). The prevalence and correlates of eating disorders in the National Comorbidity Survey Replication [Electronic version]. *Biological Psychiatry 61*(3), 348–58.

Chapter 10 *Planning*

1. Ziglar, Z. (2005). *See you at the top*. Gretna, LA: Pelican Publishing Company.

2. U.S. Census Bureau. (2008). What it's worth: Field of training and economic status in 2004. *Facts for features*. Retrieved May 22, 2009, from http://www.census.gov/Press-Release/www/releases/archives/cb08ff-12.pdf
   Data tables are available from U.S. Census Bureau, Survey of Income and Program Participation, 2004 Panel. Retrieved May 22, 2009 from http://www.census.gov/population/www/socdemo/education/sipp2004w2.html

INDEX

S

T

V

W